Warren Marcus has the heartbeat of God. All of creation is shouting, "It's time to have experiential knowledge of God the Father." This is a how-to book. It will prepare you for the next and greatest and perhaps last move of God's Spirit.

—Sid Israel Roth
Host, *It's Supernatural!*

Warren Marcus has written a fascinating study on the Priestly Blessing that helps Christians understand the significance of the Father's blessing. As a Jewish believer Warren takes us back to the Jewish roots of the Christian faith. He focuses on the fullness of the Godhead (Elohim) to help us understand the magnitude of God's person and the significance of His blessings in our lives. Don't miss this incredible book!

—Dr. Ed Hindson
Founding Dean and Distinguished Professor,
Rawlings School of Divinity Liberty University

Many books have been written on how to obtain an intimate relationship with Jesus through the born again experience. Other books have been published sharing how to enter into a powerful relationship with the person of the Holy Spirit through the baptism of the Holy Spirit. Warren Marcus, a Jewish believer in Jesus as his Messiah and Lord, has been given new insight on how to enter into a supernatural, experiential, and intimate relationship with the heavenly Father. He has been given the keys to unlock the power behind the only prayer written by God Himself in the entire Bible, the Aaronic Blessing. He uncovers the fullness of meaning conveyed from the original Hebrew and shares how to pronounce this prayer over yourself and others in the manner God Himself intended. I highly suggest you read this powerful book.

—Pat Robertson
Founder/Chairman, Christian Broadcasting Network Inc.

*The Priestly Prayer of the Blessing* is a fascinating reading experience. The non-Jewish reader will be immersed into the world of Jewish cultures and traditions. The Jewish events are included in explanations of Jewish phrases, which will expand the understanding of the reader. But also the Hebrew spellings of the names of the Father, the Son, and the Holy Spirit will grab the attention of readers because the unusual focus and attention on the object of the words, God Himself. Warren Marcus is my friend. We have prayed together and served the Lord together at Thomas Road Baptist Church and Liberty University. May the testimony of his conversion experience capture your heart. Perhaps you might share this book with Jewish friends—that could lead to their accepting Jesus as their Messiah and Lord.

—Dr. Elmer L. Towns
Cofounder and Vice President, Liberty University

As I read this book, I became overwhelmed by the rich revelation relating to the Hebrew meaning of the words in this Priestly Blessing. The blessing in Numbers 6 has been very significant in my life, but reading this powerful book has given me fresh revelation of the Father's extravagant love and care for us. After I finished reading this book, I was compelled to kneel, pray, worship, and take time to apply what I had read and received, thanking God for His blessing and kindness. I pray that this book will take you into deeper fellowship with the Father and provoke you to worship, just as it has done for me.

—Katherine Ruonala
Author, Living in the Miraculous, Wilderness to Wonder,
and Life With the Holy Spirit
Senior Leader, Glory City Church Brisbane and Glory
City Network

Warren Marcus, as a five-year-old Jewish boy, had an extraordinary dream about visiting heaven and seeing the God of Israel in the form of the Shekinah glory. In his book, The Priestly Prayer of the Blessing, Warren shares how this dream was the catalyst that began his fascinating journey to find and truly know God in a supernatural, experiential, and intimate way! Ultimately his book conveys how we can truly access our heavenly Father in a tangible, powerful way! This book unveils the deeper meaning of the prayer that the high priest Aaron would pronounce over the children of Israel every day while they wandered in the wilderness. Warren was given a revelation of the fullness of the meaning of this prayer as expressed in the Hebrew. His findings will fascinate you and profoundly affect you as you sense the heavenly Father's love for you and as you access the Father's divine embrace! Many books have been written on the "Father heart" of God, but this book by Warren Marcus is not just knowing about our heavenly Father and His character, but instead it's about Warren's discovery on how to actually access our heavenly Father in a supernatural, experiential, and intimate way. I highly recommend reading this powerful and engaging book.

—JOSEPH FARAH
FOUNDER AND CHIEF EXECUTIVE OFFICER, WND.COM,
WND BOOKS, WND FILMS

Years ago in the mid '60s, when I was a newly recommitted, on-fire Christian, I liked to listen to a dear Jewish radio evangelist named Dr. Arthur Michelson, who was faithfully preaching the gospel of Jesus Christ. He would always end his broadcast with Numbers 6:24–26: "The LORD bless you and keep you; the LORD make His face shine upon you, and be gracious to you; the LORD lift up His countenance upon you, and give you peace." And then he would add, "In Jesus's name, amen!" I always appreciated the special blessing as his program ended.

Warren Marcus tells of how in a recent archaeological dig in the old city of David, in Jerusalem, a small silver scroll was found with this very prayer inscribed in Paleo-Hebrew. It was from the tomb of an ancient high priest of Israel. The prayer was powerful then, and it is powerful still today. The scripture Numbers 6:27 goes on to say that when you put the LORD's name on His people, He will bless them!

In his new book, *The Priestly Prayer of the Blessing*, Warren tells how you can experience the power of this prayer over your life and family. May you be abundantly blessed as you read about it and receive your supernatural blessing that your heavenly Father intends for you to receive.

—JOHN ARNOTT
CATCH THE FIRE MINISTRIES
TORONTO, CANADA

If you desire to experience the fatherhood of God in a fresh and powerful way, this book is for you. Warren has revealed ancient secrets that will usher the church into the Shekinah glory of God. As you read each page, open your heart to receive supernatural downloads directly from God's heart to yours. You will discover the true meaning of the Aaronic Blessing and how to release God's power in your life.

—Dr. Kynan Bridges
Best-Selling Author, *School of the Presence*
CEO, Kynan Bridges Ministries Inc.

At age five Warren Marcus was visited by God in a dream and experienced a measure of the glory. God saw that if He revealed Himself, Warren would respond to the Father and pursue His person and His heart!

This book is born of a God-given passion to know the Father and make Him known through Jesus (Yeshua) the Messiah! The heavenly Father has been looking for someone to make Him known like He has never been known before in this critical hour. We are in a time of transition, and the major key to both personal and church transformation is coming to know the very One, Jesus (Yeshua), who came to manifest both the person and the glory of the Father Himself.

If you are one who is hungry for more of God, this book is for you! You have experienced the Holy Spirit and the Lord Jesus, but this revelation will take you into the experience of the Father Himself and your Father hunger will be satisfied! In the pages of this book you will find the life, the light, and the love of the Father!

—Pastor Tony Kemp
Tony Kemp Ministries

The Priestly Blessing, found in the book of Numbers, is the only prayer that places the very name of God upon us. Warren Marcus, a Jewish believer in Jesus for more than four decades, shares prophetic insight that will bless you, your family, and all those you love.

—Jonathan Bernis
Host, *Jewish Voice With Jonathan Bernis*

As Jesus was being lifted up to heaven, He raised His hands and blessed His disciples (Luke 24:50). In this book Warren Marcus reveals the Hebrew meaning of the words Jesus used and how you can access the same blessing. Today and every day, you can have the power of His name and be confident that you have the blessing of God.

—Gordon Robertson
CEO, Christian Broadcasting Network

If prayer has always been a mystery to you, this book will open the secrets you've been searching for. Warren Marcus has discovered what the ancient priests prayed to receive heaven's blessings, power, and presence. Now you, through the teaching of this book, can experience the same divine glory by speaking the ancient Priestly Prayer over your own life. Warren has written a timely book that is easy to understand and, if rightly applied, could change your life forever.

—Steve Gray
Senior Pastor, World Revival Church of Kansas City
(Smithton Outpouring)

Your heart will be stirred and your faith inspired, just as mine were, when you read the unfolding of the precious revelation that G-D has given Warren. It was my joy to be there when Warren Marcus first met His Messiah in October 1974. Hallelujah!

—James Tate
Pastor Emeritus, Calvary Tabernacle

# TESTIMONIES

I have personally been blessed by proclaiming this Priestly Prayer of the Blessing over myself and family. Every day we air the prayer sung in Hebrew over our audience with the video piece produced by Warren Marcus. Many watching have ordered the course and the pendant.

—Dorothy Spaulding
President and Founder, Watchmen Broadcasting

Faced with losing my home, I began proclaiming the Priestly Prayer of the Blessing every day. A woman in my church gave me twenty thousand dollars, which was the exact amount needed to rescue my home. In addition, a friend unexpectedly bought me new tires for my car, including road hazard coverage, which I desperately needed.

—Lynda Sullivan

I pray the Priestly Prayer of the Blessing every day, and the sweet blessings that God wants to bestow upon my life are experienced daily. I speak the verses out of God's holy Word and then speak the amplified Hebrew-to-English translation. My walk and faith in God has become stronger; my passion and desire for Him has become greater. I have seen God bless my life and my family's life. My dad was diagnosed with multiple myeloma (cancer of the bone). And praise be to our God Almighty and our soon and coming King, my dad was touched by the Master's hand and is fully and completely healed. I was laid off from a great paying job and needed work, and God has blessed me with two different jobs. In praying this divine prayer over my life daily, it has made me capable to stand firmly in boldness and proclaim "His sweet name" and have the courage to speak out and not be in fear of making a mistake or saying the wrong thing. I have always been a shy person, but God has enabled me to be bold!

—Sharon K. Barr

The revelation of the Priestly Prayer of the Blessing that the God of Israel has imparted to Warren Marcus has made a profound impact on my life. I believe this revelation is a prophetic release of the power of embracing the fullness of Elohim and the understanding that the one true God is the God of Israel. Those who worship Him and receive the blessing bear His name. This name is obvious to the entire spirit realm and is the anointing of walking in His favor and His authority. Not only is "Abba, Father God," more fully understood, the glory of Yeshua, our great High Priest, is also revealed because He has made those who believe in Him priests forever after the order of Melchizedek. This gives us the blessing of receiving this prayer from Him and also the authority to pray it ourselves over others as His priesthood. As we fully receive, embrace, and then impart this divine prayer in the amplified Hebrew-to-English translation, we proclaim the glory of Elohim (one true G-D of Israel).

—Cathy Hargett
Founder, Highway to Zion Ministries

There were people who were coming against our reputation and spreading false things about us, but after proclaiming the Priestly Prayer, this stopped. We were also facing sleepless nights, but now we are able to get a good night's sleep every night! And last of all, we were struggling with our finances, but after proclaiming the divine prayer every day, we now have to turn down bookings because we can't keep up with all of them.

—The Chrisagis Brothers (Brian and Shawn)
Christian Recording Artists

I feel so blessed to have been able to have Warren Marcus bless Paris Presbyterian Church with his amazing teaching and anointed ministry. So many times when I feel lost or under attack, I listen to his teaching on this prayer, and it brings peace to my soul. I pray the amplified version of the Priestly Prayer of the Blessing every day. Thank you, Warren, for explaining the meaning in such great detail. I thank God for Warren explaining the meaning in such great detail.

—Margie Kasper Zellars
Director of Outreach, Paris Presbyterian Church

# THE
# PRIESTLY
# PRAYER OF THE
# BLESSING

## WARREN M. MARCUS

CHARISMA
HOUSE

Most CHARISMA HOUSE BOOK GROUP products are available at special quantity discounts for bulk purchase for sales promotions, premiums, fund-raising, and educational needs. For details, write Charisma House Book Group, 600 Rinehart Road, Lake Mary, Florida 32746, or telephone (407) 333-0600.

THE PRIESTLY PRAYER OF THE BLESSING by Warren M. Marcus
Published by Charisma House
Charisma Media/Charisma House Book Group
600 Rinehart Road
Lake Mary, Florida 32746
www.charismahouse.com

Cover design by Vincent Pirozzi
Design Director: Justin Evans

Visit the author's website at www.WarrenMarcus.com.

Library of Congress Cataloging-in-Publication Data:
An application to register this book for cataloging has been submitted to the Library of Congress.
International Standard Book Number: 978-1-62999-491-8
E-book ISBN: 978-1-62999-492-5

18 19 20 21 22 — 1098765432
Printed in the United States of America

This book might be the most important book you will ever read next to the Bible itself. How can I make such a bold claim? I can because this book contains the only prayer from the entire Bible that the one true G-D of Israel wrote. This divine prayer of blessing was not just meant for the children of Israel, but it is given for us today. You will learn the secret of how to access its supernatural power!

I want to honor my wife, Donna, my son, Joseph, and my daughter, Tara, for their prayers and support.

Special thanks to my mentors: Pastor James Tate, Sid Israel Roth, and Rick Amato (who encouraged me to pursue the meaning of the Priestly Prayer of the Blessing for us today).

I dedicate this book in memory of my Messianic Jewish mother, Pearl Marcus, who went home to be with the Lord at the age of 104.

# CONTENTS

# "G-D" AND THE
# MYSTERY OF THE DASH!

In THIS BOOK you will notice that I refer to God as G-D and also YHWH. I was torn about using G-D versus God and also YHWH. In addition I struggled with the use of *Yeshua* (Jesus) and *Ruach HaKodesh* (Holy Spirit). My publisher and I wondered if Christians would stumble over these Hebrew names. But I felt a strong leading that this is to be a teachable moment for the church, and I believe the Lord showed me something.

When Mel Gibson produced *The Passion of the Christ*, he chose to have the actors speak the language of that time—Hebrew, Aramaic, and Latin—and use subtitles! Others counseled him that this was a bad idea because it would get in the way of people watching the movie. They pleaded with him to just do it in English. But he didn't listen, and it wound up being one of the most successful Christian motion pictures of all time!

If the movie had been in English, perhaps the words spoken would have sounded simple and hokey! It would have been just another Christian movie. But by using the actual languages of the life and times of Yeshua instead, it added to the authenticity and the supernatural power of the biblical story so that the audience ultimately had a different experience, which I believe was intended by God Himself.

I shared this with my publisher and explained that concerning *The Priestly Prayer of the Blessing* I felt led to refer to God as G-D. We decided this note to explain the reasoning behind the unusual reference would help to clear things up for readers.

## WHY OMIT THE VOWEL *O*?

Though I was born and raised in a completely Jewish home and then in 1974 received Yeshua as my Messiah and Lord, I don't normally spell God as G-D. I'm very familiar with the fact that religious Jewish people are taught to respect and honor the one true G-D of Israel in this fashion for reasons you might not fully understand, but I will explain more thoroughly in this book.

One key reason is because this spelling refers back to the *tetragrammaton*, which depicts in Hebrew the sacred name of the one true G-D of Israel, which He gave to Moses in the *Torah*. The tetragrammaton contains only the consonants of G-D's sacred name and is expressed as Y-H-W-H.

The vowels are missing so the actual pronunciation of His sacred name is not fully known. Scholars can only speculate. The sacred name refers specifically to the heavenly Father! This book is about the person of the heavenly Father making Himself known to us in an intimate, supernatural, and experiential way!

I am not asking anyone to refer this way to G-D, but again I believe this is a teachable moment.

When we as believers say we believe or trust in God, how do others interpret this? They may think we are telling about Krishna, Buddha, or some other god. But when one sees "G-D," it unmistakably refers to the one and only true God of Israel.

A newborn baby doesn't understand where the source of the mother's milk would come from until the mother introduces the baby to her breast. Once the baby makes the connection, not only is the baby fed, but also a unique and precious relationship between the mother and child is established. This book introduces the reader to a new and life-changing relationship with the heavenly Father as He makes Himself available to us in a way that's tangible.

I believe this is the time when the heavenly Father is going to make Himself known to the church in a way like never before. I believe this book is a tool He will use to help accomplish this purpose. As you read this book, every time you see our heavenly Father referred to as G-D or YHWH, my prayer is that it will be a continual reminder to you that He is seeking to reveal Himself to you in a new and deeper way. Like the hidden letters in the name, there are parts of our heavenly Father that are waiting to be revealed to you as you seek a deeper, more intimate relationship with Him. It is not just knowing who our heavenly Father is; it's getting to know Him intimately, supernaturally, and experientially in the manner He always intended!

# PREFACE

WHAT IF THE one true G-D of Israel actually wrote a prayer that *He* wanted to be proclaimed over *you* every day that would bring supernatural favor, prosperity, abundance, healing, better relationships, protection, order, rest, wisdom, blessings, miracles, and so much more?

This supernatural prayer wouldn't be based on how good or perfect you are; it would be so powerful that through its daily proclamation over you the one true G-D of Israel would give you power to choose that which is good and would help you to make godly decisions. The supernatural power of this prayer would propel you to be successful in all your endeavors.

The truth is G-D did write such a prayer!

## THROUGH THIS BOOK YOU WILL...

+ Understand the full meaning of this ancient prayer and unlock its supernatural power!

+ Discover the secret of proclaiming an amplified Hebrew-to-English translation over yourself and others every day!

+ Receive through this anointed prayer everything you need to walk in supernatural health, provision, protection, peace, and so much more to fulfill your God-given destiny!

You will also learn that the real, tangible, supernatural impartation comes only after you do three key things that are unveiled in this book.

1. Learn the secret of how to proclaim this prayer in a manner G-D Himself intended it to be pronounced.

2. Proclaim the amplified Hebrew-to-English prayer over yourself every day!

3. After you have proclaimed the prayer over yourself, listen to the prayer being sung over you in Hebrew by the world-renowned Messianic worship leader Paul Wilbur. Visit www.WarrenMarcus.com/prayer to access this anointed Hebrew version of the prayer in either audio or video form. Both formats have been provided as a way to bless you in a powerful way.

*Please don't read these three simple steps and think that this is a magic trick or cheap gimmick. Quite the opposite is true.* The Jewish high priest Aaron chanted the Priestly Prayer of the Blessing in Hebrew every day over the children of Israel when they were in the wilderness. It contains a very rich and deep impartation from our heavenly Father, and I am passionate about sharing it with you because I believe it can truly change your life.

I've shared the truths contained in this book with groups of Baptists, Presbyterians, Methodists, Charismatics, Catholics, and even Jewish people, and every time the same thing happens! The awesome, tangible presence of the *Elohim* (the triune nature of G-D) begins to impact everyone in the room.

This Priestly Prayer of the Blessing has radically changed my life and what I experience every day by His power. In fact, I continually receive testimonies of believers who have experienced the supernatural power of this Priestly Prayer of the Blessing and are seeing miracles happen on a regular basis.

Will you join me for an in-depth exploration of the Priestly Prayer of the Blessing?

I pray you will!

—WARREN M. MARCUS

# SECTION I:
# THE JOURNEY BEGINS!

# Chapter 1

# AN AMAZING DISCOVERY

O̶N A FRIDAY morning in the spring of 2013 I was working in my office and my cell phone rang with a call from an unknown number. I was reluctant to answer it. But something deep inside me telegraphed the importance of the call. It was from Rick Amato, one of my closest brothers in Messiah (Christ)—a mentor and the main person responsible for my ordination as a "Messianic Jewish Southern Baptist evangelist"! (That's a story for another book!) Rick has personally met with Russian presidents Gorbachev and Yeltsin and conducted the first—and one of the *only*—gospel preaching crusades in the Kremlin. In my estimation, and that of a host of others, Rick is one of greatest preachers of our time. More than one million souls can be credited to coming into the kingdom of G-D through his ministry! In addition, long before the opiate crisis, he founded WaronAddiction.com in 1993 and has reached one million children in the United States of America. More important to me, Rick has always held a deep love for the one true G-D of Israel and His holy Word.

Rick was calling from Jerusalem, Israel, and he was quite emotional. He was deeply overcome by something that had just happened to him. He had been with an agnostic Jewish archaeologist, Gabriel Barkay, on the site where two silver amulets (pendants) were discovered in 1979 and 1981. The archaeological site was located in the City of David in Jerusalem near the Temple Mount in what was believed to be the tomb of a Jewish high priest. (I've included photos of the amulets and the site in the photo section of this book.) The two amulets have been certifiably dated as being from the late seventh century BC.[1]

These amulets were found in the fourth of several burial caves. Each amulet was a rolled-up sheet of silver, which when carefully unrolled over a three-year period, revealed a passage of Scripture found in the Torah and referred to as the "Priestly Benediction" or the "Priestly Prayer of the Blessing." The inscription, etched into the silver, is four hundred years older than the Hebrew writings found on the sacred Dead Sea Scrolls. In other words, it is the oldest evidence of Scripture in existence![2]

Rick shared, "Warren, do you know how significant this discovery is? It's the oldest evidence of an intact Holy Bible scripture."

When he said that, it startled me. I began to wonder, "Why did G-D preserve this particular portion of the Scriptures? Why have these amulets been discovered in this period of history if it wasn't significant for this dispensation of time we are living in?"

Rick continued, "This Prayer of the Blessing is one that was given directly by G-D to Moses. Moses was instructed that when the high priest of Israel, Aaron, would proclaim it over the children of Israel every day, it would result in G-D placing His very name upon them."

I tried to fully grasp what Rick was communicating. He was so overcome with emotion.

With a trembling voice Rick continued, "The writing etched on the silver amulets is in the ancient Paleo-Hebrew." He reminded me that in our English Bibles, this Priestly Prayer of the Blessing is found in Numbers 6:24–26:

> The LORD bless you and keep you; the LORD make His face to shine upon you, and be gracious unto you; the LORD lift His countenance upon you, and give you peace.

"But," Rick explained, "the name of the one true G-D of Israel etched into the silver amulet was not the Hebrew word *Adonai*, which is translated as *Lord* in English. It is the tetragrammaton— the Hebrew consonants: Yod-Hey-Vav-Hey (YHWH). The vowels of G-D's sacred Hebrew name are missing. The exact pronunciation is a mystery. The tetragrammaton refers to the sacred name of G-D that only the high priest of Israel could pronounce because it has been considered too holy for anyone else to utter." (I'll discuss this more in a later chapter.)

Rick was now unashamedly weeping as he continued, "I was so overcome by the historical significance of this discovery, I fell to my knees on the ground by the cave where the amulets were discovered, and I began to pray. Gabriel Barkay placed the first replica of the real amulet upon my neck." He shared that the original amulets were in a museum in Israel.

Rick continued, "Warren, I started shaking as Gabriel placed the amulet on me. And then he pronounced the words of the blessing over me in Hebrew. It was then that I could feel the power of the name come upon me like hot oil being poured over my head and flowing down my entire body. I will never be the same again!"

I was having trouble fully connecting to Rick's passionate and emotion-laden communication. I thought, "I am a Jew, and Rick is a Gentile, yet it was he who was in Israel being immersed in this supernatural encounter with the Most High G-D."

In the New Testament epistle to the Romans the Jewish apostle Paul said,

> So I say, have they {Israel} stumbled so as to fall [to spiritual ruin]? Certainly not! But by their transgression [their rejection of the Messiah] salvation has come to the Gentiles, to make Israel jealous [when they realize what they have forfeited].
> —Romans 11:11, AMP

Rick, a Gentile believer, was doing his job by making me, the Jew, jealous! When I hung up, I immediately turned in my Bible to read the text of Numbers 6:24–26 for myself. I even spoke it out loud over myself with all the passion I could muster. Frankly I didn't sense anything unusual. As a matter of fact, I have heard this prayer proclaimed over me in various Messianic and even Gentile church services. Though I felt it was a beautiful prayer, it didn't impact me like it appeared to do for Rick Amato.

Others have told me that their priest in a Catholic, Anglican, or Episcopal church pronounced this prayer over them. Still others experienced this prayer being proclaimed over them in their Protestant churches.

Growing up as a Jewish boy, I cannot recall the rabbi in our conservative synagogue ever pronouncing this blessing over us. If he did, it wasn't a high point of the Shabbat service. I don't believe my rabbi understood the powerful significance of this priestly prayer and how to proclaim it over his congregation in the manner G-D Himself intended.

I have known Jewish people and even some Christians who have pronounced this prayer over their children. But I sensed from Rick that something far more powerful occurred with him concerning this divine prayer—something that shook him to his core!

Then I remembered what Rick said, "When the high priest of Israel, Aaron, proclaimed it over the people, G-D said it would result in the placing of His very name upon them." I looked in my Bible again and the words immediately following the Priestly Prayer of the Blessing in the next verse popped out. This verse declares that as a result of this divine prayer being proclaimed over the children of Israel, "they [the high priest of Israel and his successors] will put [actually be placing] My name upon the children of Israel, and I [G-D] will bless them" (Num. 6:27).

It is apparent that this had larger implications than I comprehended. I thought, "If this is as significant as Rick Amato was trying to communicate, then what happened to the children of Israel when it was proclaimed over them by the high priest Aaron?"

When I researched the facts, I was stunned! As a result of this being proclaimed over them by the high priest every day for forty years in the wilderness, the following took place:

+ They received daily provision—*manna* from heaven— and when they got tired of eating manna, G-D sent them quail!

+ They received divine angelic protection from their enemies!

+ They had supernatural health!

+ They had supernatural wealth—their flocks increased. Even in the desert the animals had plenty to eat!

+ For forty years their sandals and their clothing never wore out!

+ Their population multiplied with the blessing of more children!

+ The Shekinah glory of G-D (His actual awesome presence) would come into the holy of holies in the midst of the camp!

+ Whenever there was a problem, Moses would go into the cloud of the Shekinah glory to meet with G-D and ask for His wisdom—His solution to problems—and every time G-D would answer his prayers!

+ They had "supernatural air conditioning"—a supernatural cloud by day would cover the entire camp (the entire population of Israel), and it would bring the temperature down during the hot desert days!

+ They had "supernatural heating" too—a supernatural pillar of fire would extend over the entire camp, giving them heat to keep them warm from the cold desert nights!

These miracles happened for the entire forty years in the desert as a result of the Priestly Prayer of the Blessing being proclaimed over them every day. This was astounding! Again I wondered why it didn't appear to have the same supernatural power when declared over me by a rabbi or a minister from a church or when I pronounced it over myself.

I then realized something quite profound about this passage in the Bible. The children of Israel had just begged Aaron to make a golden calf for them to worship since they feared that Moses had disappeared during his forty days and nights on Mount Sinai.

While Moses was meeting with the one true G-D of Israel to receive the Ten Commandments written by G-D's own finger, the children of Israel began worshipping the golden calf. They did not deserve to have G-D's very name placed upon them. For G-D to not abandon them and instead choose to bless the children of Israel means that this has to be the greatest prayer of grace contained in the Bible. Again, the thought came to mind that this is the only prayer in the entire Bible authored by the G-D of Israel Himself.

I thought, "Of all the scriptures in the Bible, why would the one true G-D of Israel preserve this ancient prayer as being the oldest intact scripture (found on those amulets), predating the sacred Dead Sea scrolls by four hundred years, if it didn't have a deeper implication for us today?"

Until now I had never considered its significance. The two amulets are collecting dust in a museum, and yet this is the most significant

biblical and archaeological discovery ever! Through the pronouncement of this divine prayer every day over the children of Israel they
obtained an impartation of G-D's presence and benefited from the
supernatural power of the greatest prayer of grace contained in the
Holy Scriptures.

I wondered, "Could it be that the one true G-D of Israel wanted us
to have this rediscovered today because we are living in the end times?
Could it be that now is the time in history that He wants the Priestly
Prayer of the Blessing revealed to bless those who believe in Him?"

It still puzzled me that Rick was so overwhelmed by this Priestly
Prayer of the Blessing as it was proclaimed over him, but when I read
the prayer and tried to proclaim it over myself, it didn't have any
effect on me. I beseeched the Lord, "Please tell me, Lord, what is the
truth about Your Priestly Prayer of the Blessing?"

Then something Rick said came to my remembrance. "I knelt on
the ground in front of Gabriel Barkay. I started shaking as Gabriel
placed that amulet on me and then he pronounced the words of the
blessing over me in Hebrew."

A number of questions flooded my mind. Was it because Rick was
so near the place of discovery of the amulets? Was there a special portal,
a doorway, to heaven in that place? Could the power be in the amulet
itself? What does it mean that the one true G-D of Israel placed His
name on the children of Israel? Why was Moses told to have Aaron
the high priest and his successors pronounce this over the children of
Israel and not Moses? What about the fact that the Priestly Prayer of
the Blessing was said over Rick in Hebrew and not English?

These questions and so many more began to consume me. Thus
began my deep search into the truth about this Priestly Prayer of the
Blessing. What was revealed to me has literally transformed my own
life and the lives of many others. The key was in understanding the
full meaning conveyed in the ancient Hebrew and how to proclaim
it over oneself and others in the manner that G-D Himself intended.
This resulted in unlocking the supernatural power of this Priestly
Prayer of the Blessing for us today.

## Where the Power Comes From

Did the power come from the fact that my friend Rick knelt on the
very location where the amulets were discovered?

As I began my search into the secret behind this divine prayer, I quickly discerned that the location of the discovery of the amulets had no special significance concerning what Rick experienced. How do I know this? Because in my studies I found that places deemed holy (set apart) in the Bible are revered because the presence of G-D was once revealed in that location. Thus, from that point of time in history, these locations were held in high esteem as "places of remembrance," but the actual ground itself had no supernatural value without the presence. When G-D revealed Himself to Moses in the burning bush, it became holy ground because His presence was there. The bush itself held no special power.

The Holy Land itself is reverenced because in the Bible G-D states that this land is His land. It's where He revealed Himself and where Yeshua (Jesus), His only begotten Son, was born. It is the place where someday soon the one true G-D of Israel and the Lamb, Yeshua, will return, literally bringing heaven onto the earth.

> And I John saw the holy city, new Jerusalem, coming down from [G-D the heavenly Father] out of heaven, prepared as a bride adorned for her husband. And I heard a great voice out of heaven saying, Behold, the tabernacle of [G-D the heavenly Father] is with men, and he will dwell with them, and they shall be his people, and [G-D] himself shall be with them, and be their [G-D the heavenly Father].
>
> —Revelation 21:2–3, kjv

> And I saw no temple therein: for the Lord [G-D] Almighty [the heavenly Father] and the Lamb [Yeshua Jesus] are the temple of it. And the city had no need of the sun, neither of the moon, to shine in it: for the glory of [G-D the heavenly Father] did lighten it, and the Lamb is the light [the lampstand] thereof.
>
> —Revelation 21:22–23, kjv

According to the Word of G-D, Jerusalem is holy (set apart) as the city of G-D. One day soon it shall be truly holy because the one true G-D of Israel Himself (the heavenly Father) along with Yeshua will come down from heaven and abide in New Jerusalem.

Note in the above verses that there is a distinction between G-D the heavenly Father and His Son, Yeshua. They will both be manifested on earth in New Jerusalem.

And the nations of those who are saved shall walk in its light, and the kings of the earth shall bring their glory and honor into it. Its gates shall never be shut by day, for there shall be no night there. They shall bring into it the glory and honor of the nations. No unclean thing shall ever enter it, nor shall anyone who commits abomination or falsehood, but only those whose names are written in the Lamb's Book of Life.

—Revelation 21:24–27

Where did the power come from that affected my friend Rick? Was it in the amulet?

I am certain the power was not in the amulet when it was placed upon Rick's neck. So many hold on to items as holy icons. Religion often promotes and cherishes articles they consider sacred. Unfortunately icons are looked upon as idols or magic charms to be cherished, worshipped, and considered to bring good luck, when they should be considered only as reminders of the reality of the one true G-D of Israel.

Every day I wear the authorized silver-plated replica of the Priestly Prayer of the Blessing amulet on my neck. (See photo section.) It's just like the one placed on Rick Amato that day as he knelt by the cave where it was discovered. Etched on the front of it is the ancient Paleo-Hebrew of this supernatural prayer, a facsimile of how it appears on the original. On the back is the Priestly Prayer of the Blessing inscribed in English. I wear it as a witness and a reminder of the power of this divine prayer. There is nothing holy about the pendant. The power is in the Priestly Prayer of the Blessing.

I believe the greatest significance of the ancient amulet's discovery lies in the fact that the Paleo-Hebrew writing etched in silver is the oldest evidence of Holy Scripture we have in the world today. Even more important is the fact that the one true G-D of Israel chose to preserve this particular portion of the Holy Scriptures. But why? Perhaps because until now no one considered that this one prayer is the *only* prayer authored by G-D Himself.

I believe that G-D has preserved this particular portion of the Holy Scripture because He has a special purpose for this prayer for such a time as this. Again, I emphasize that the power is in the Priestly Prayer of the Blessing itself. I truly believe that once you discover the full meaning of the prayer and understand how to pronounce the prayer over yourself and others as G-D intended it to be proclaimed, your life will never be the same!

## G-D's PRAYER OF GRACE (UNMERITED FAVOR) IN THE DESERT

As slaves in Egypt, what the children of Israel knew concerning the one true G-D was limited to oral histories passed down through the centuries from their forefathers. They didn't yet have the inspired Word of G-D, the Bible, to teach them who G-D truly was. The Torah had not yet been given by G-D to Moses. They had no real clue as to who the G-D of Israel truly was.

When G-D began to perform the miracles and wonders that led to Israel's freedom, they must have wondered who this powerful G-D was. They were frightened by this entity who had power to send ten horrible plagues upon Egypt, the One who parted the Red Sea and destroyed the Egyptian army. They weren't comforted but rather they were frightened because they hadn't encountered the reality of His power and presence.

Armed with the hope of a Promised Land flowing with milk and honey, the children of Israel crossed the Red Sea. Imagine their disappointment when all they found on the other side was endless desert.

The children of Israel had little understanding concerning the G-D who led them out of Egypt. They had little cognizance of the fact that they—the Hebrews enslaved by Egypt who were now free—were the physical descendants of Abraham. The Old Testament had not yet been written—Moses was about to receive the first five books, the Torah, from the one true G-D of Israel on Mount Sinai.

They beheld ten plagues that were unleashed upon Pharaoh and Egypt for not letting them go free. They witnessed G-D parting the Red Sea and holding back the Egyptian army with a pillar of fire from heaven. They walked on dry ground as G-D made a pathway between two walls of raging water. And when they got to the other side, they watched as G-D caused the water to come crashing down upon the Egyptian army who was pursuing them with a vengeance.

Yet, while Moses was meeting with G-D on Mount Sinai receiving His Word—His instructions, the Torah—they had Aaron build a golden calf and began worshipping this idol. Moses was meeting with

G-D on the top of Mount Sinai receiving the Ten Commandments written by G-D's own finger, carved in stone.

G-D was angry with the children of Israel for worshipping the golden calf in the valley below. He told Moses that He was going to "wipe them out"—but Moses interceded, and G-D repented of His anger against them.

It was to this rebellious, imperfect people, the children of Israel, that the one true G-D gave this supernatural prayer, the Priestly Prayer of the Blessing, for them to experience His reality in a personal and powerful way. G-D would soon tell Moses to have this prayer pronounced every day over the children of Israel by the high priest Aaron and Aaron's descendants.

Do you understand what I am saying here? This wasn't a man's prayer to G-D—this was a prayer *conceived by the G-D of Israel Himself* to be prayed over us. And it is the greatest prayer of grace ever given to mankind. It is a supernatural prayer!

The children of Israel were in the wilderness. How many of you are having a "wilderness experience" in your life? What are your needs? Are they not the same needs that the children of Israel had? For forty years this supernatural prayer was pronounced over the children of Israel, and as a result they walked in supernatural provision, health, protection, and prosperity!

I myself wandered through my own desert, being subject to the influence of the world, my own fleshly desires, and the constant assault by the enemy of my soul, Satan. I must admit that the one true G-D of Israel was consistently pursuing me. G-D sent many witnesses, circumstances, and supernatural occurrences to bring me out of the place where I had come to the end of myself.

In the next chapter I'll share a dream I had where G-D revealed Himself to me in the form of the Shekinah glory when I was a five-year-old Jewish boy. This dream set me on a journey to want to know the one true G-D of Israel in an intimate way. In October 1974, at twenty-one years of age, I sat in my apartment getting stoned on marijuana. I had come to the intellectual conclusion that Yeshua could be the promised Jewish Messiah because of the many Old Testament prophecies He clearly fulfilled. But I couldn't understand how the knowledge of that fact could impact me further. It's one thing to know *about* G-D; it is another to *know* Him in a supernatural, experiential, and intimate way. I cried out to the one true G-D of Israel with a simple prayer:

> *Oh, G-D, whoever You are, if Jesus is what the Christians say He is, the promised Jewish Messiah and the only begotten Son of G-D, then I want Him to come into my heart. If He isn't what they say He is, then I don't want anything to do with Him. You will have to let me know what the truth truly is.*

I felt a supernatural peace, and as I lifted the joint of marijuana to inhale it, I stopped. I asked myself, "Why am I doing this?" I flushed an entire bag of the drug down the toilet. I had no desire to ever use that drug again. I picked up a King James Version of the Bible I had purchased and began to read passages in the New Testament. Verses I couldn't understand before were suddenly completely understood. It's as if G-D Himself was communicating directly to me off the pages of the Bible.

I walked into my apartment office to place the Bible back onto a shelf. As I looked at the other books, I realized many of them were completely contrary to the things of G-D. No one preached to me; the sense of G-D's holiness permeated the atmosphere. I threw away many books that day, including pornography, radical political writings, and false religious and occult writings. For over a year it was as if I walked in a "honeymoon period" with the reality of G-D in my life, empowered by the Ruach HaKodesh (Holy Spirit) within to walk in holiness.

Through the years I have known many people who also had a powerful encounter with the one true G-D of Israel. Many were delivered from drug addiction, sinful lifestyles, criminal activities, and more! As time went by, some found themselves sliding backward into their former lifestyles or going through the motions of contending for the faith that once transformed them.

Although I had a powerful supernatural encounter with the one true G-D of Israel when I first recognized Yeshua as my Messiah and Lord (*Adonai*), as time went on I found myself being conformed to people who claimed to be following G-D, but their lives didn't always reflect that reality.

At one point in my journey I began to relate to others who once walked in holiness but had backslidden and were now tainted by the temptations of the world, the flesh, and the devil. Their belief was that "G-D is love and I am forgiven, so there are no rules. I can do anything because He still loves me." There is partial theological truth to this way of thinking. G-D's love for us, even when we are struggling or drifting away from Him, is ever present. But His blessings and favor come through our pursuit of an intimate relationship with Him and our desire to embrace the things He identifies as holy.

The "honeymoon period" often disappears, and in many people's lives something happens. The enemy begins to steal our joy and confidence in Him. So many people don't understand what is happening. We often feel we can relate to the children of Israel, and we can empathize with them as we find ourselves in a spiritual "desert place," a time of testing.

We can remember the hope that we once held on to as we were set free from our spiritual slavery to the devil, when we first repented and accepted by faith that Yeshua is our Messiah and Lord, when the Ruach HaKodesh was given to us to dwell within, and when we found ourselves being guided into G-D's promised land—a taste of heaven on earth. But now we are in a spiritual desert.

If you can identify with this right now, I pray that it encourages you to realize that while the children of Israel were in this desert climate of fear and discouragement, G-D had the earthly high priest pronounce the Priestly Prayer of the Blessing over them.

There is something special that happens when this divine prayer is either spoken or sung over people in the Hebrew language. That's because the Hebrew words have layers of meaning that are missing when the prayer is translated into English or any other language. When this prayer was said over the children of Israel, it would cause the sacred name and the person of the G-D of Israel to be placed upon them.

## IT'S AVAILABLE TO US TODAY

There are keys to how the Priestly Prayer of the Blessing can be proclaimed effectively over us today, and each chapter of this book will reveal a key and will highlight it in a review section at the close of the chapter. The first key is realizing this Priestly Prayer of the Blessing is the only prayer written by the G-D of Israel Himself.

Many cite the Lord's Prayer in the New Testament scriptures as a prayer authored by G-D Himself. They point to the fact that Yeshua is the only begotten Son of the one true G-D of Israel. The argument is presented that since Yeshua was G-D in the form of the Messiah, when He shared that prayer, it was authored by G-D too. However, the context of the Lord's Prayer was to teach us a method of how to pray to the one true G-D of Israel.

> Therefore pray in this manner: Our Father who is in heaven, hallowed be Your name. Your kingdom come; Your will be done on earth, as it is in heaven. Give us this day our daily bread. And forgive us our debts, as we forgive our debtors. And lead us not into temptation, but deliver us from evil. For Yours is the kingdom and the power and the glory forever. Amen.
>
> —Matthew 6:9–13

The prayer that Yeshua shared starts out by showing to whom we direct our prayers. He directed us to the one true G-D of Israel. Note also that Yeshua says, "Hallowed [or holy] be Your name." It is important to recognize that there is only one true G-D and Yeshua makes reference to the sacred name of that one true G-D. (More about the sacred name of G-D later in the book.)

My point is that the Lord's Prayer is Yeshua's example of how to model our prayers. He said, "Pray in this manner." It is not the same as the Priestly Prayer of the Blessing, which was authored by the one true G-D of Israel Himself and was given by Him to be proclaimed as it is written for a specific purpose.

I can't overstate the depth of this truth: G-D actually wrote this divine prayer, and He wants it to be proclaimed over you every day. I trust that as it has done for me and so many others, it will bring you supernatural favor, prosperity, abundance, healing, better relationships, blessings, miracles, and much more.

The prayer isn't based on how good or how perfect you are. The children of Israel weren't deserving of this, and neither are we. But this supernatural prayer was so powerful that it caused Israel to experience supernatural favor and blessing from G-D for forty years as they wandered in the wilderness. The supernatural result of this prayer when proclaimed over you will help propel you to be successful in all your endeavors.

Get ready, because I am going to share with you everything I learned about the deeper meaning of this supernatural prayer of grace given to us by G-D Himself.

## KEYS TO THE BLESSING

We must realize that this Priestly Prayer of the Blessing is the *only* prayer written by the G-D of Israel Himself.

## STUDY QUESTIONS

Where was Rick Amato when the Priestly Prayer of the Blessing was pronounced over him?

_____

_____

_____

What was placed on Rick Amato's neck before the prayer was administered?

_____

_____

_____

What supernatural occurrences happened to Israel during their forty years in the wilderness as a result of this divine prayer being pronounced over them every day?

_____

_____

_____

Did the amulets discovered by Gabriel Barkay in 1979–1981 have any supernatural power?

_____

_____

_____

Do the places considered to be holy sites have any supernatural power today?

_____

_____

_____

Who wrote the Priestly Prayer of the Blessing?

[ ] Moses    [ ] Aaron    [ ] Jesus    [ ] G-D

## PRAYER

*Oh, G-D of Israel, I am hungry to know You in a more intimate way than ever before. If this divine prayer that You wrote can help me experience You in a greater way, then I want You to make this real to me. Give me the ability, by the power of the Ruach HaKodesh (Holy Spirit), to understand the truth and receive an impartation of Your actual presence like never before! I pray this in the name of Yeshua (Jesus).*

# Chapter 2

# WHY ME?

I REMIND YOU THAT the book you are holding in your hands might be the most important book you will ever read—next to the Bible itself. The reason I can make this bold claim is because it contains the only prayer in the entire Bible that the one true G-D of Israel wrote and the secret of how to pronounce it over yourself and others in a manner that will allow you to access all the blessings of promises of G-D. Before I share the deeper truths about the prayer itself and how it has transformed my own life, I feel it is necessary to share how humbled and perplexed I am that the one true G-D of Israel would allow me to be the one to impart this truth.

I went through a period of asking the Lord, "Why me? Why did You choose me to impart this powerful end-time truth about Your prayer?" Through this period of deep introspection, I was taken back to the beginning of my life. Could it be that G-D prepared me before the foundation of the world to be a vessel to share this revelation for such a time as this? I don't consider myself the perfect vessel for this significant task. There are so many men and women of faith who have better credentials, notoriety, and character. Yet we know that G-D often uses the weak and foolish things of the world to confound the wise.

> But [G-D] has chosen the foolish things of the world to confound the wise. [G-D] has chosen the weak things of the world to confound the things which are mighty. And [G-D] has chosen the base things of the world and things which are despised. Yes, and He chose things which do not exist to bring to nothing things that do.
> —1 CORINTHIANS 1:27–28

So again, why me? While I pondered this question, I was taken back to my own journey of faith and was amazed to discover how G-D prepares us for our destiny and purpose while on earth.

## BROOKLYN, NEW YORK: NOVEMBER 1949

According to my parents, my *brit milah* (circumcision) took place at their apartment on Green Avenue in Brooklyn in obedience to Jewish law as written in the Torah (the five books of Moses). A large group had gathered in the tiny rooms, which were filled with the scent of cigar smoke and Scotch whiskey, and Mom says pandemonium reigned as everyone tried to outshout the others.

Dad's family was large. He had a total of ten brothers and sisters and their spouses there. Then there was my mother's side of the family, and my brother, Stan, and sister, Fran, and all the friends of the Marcus clan. The whole *mishpochah* (clan) had gathered to witness this special religious event.

The *mohel* (ritual circumciser) spoke the blessings in Hebrew and performed the circumcision. All those assembled applauded as the mohel announced that Wolf Meyer (my Yiddish/Hebrew name) was now a son of Abraham, and my name had been entered into the heavenly book as a child of Israel.

These days many Jewish people do not understand why their children are circumcised. They continue with the tradition because they feel it's the right thing to do. However, the rite is ordered by G-D Himself in the Torah as an outward sign that the child is in covenant with Him. It is the seal of the contract that binds the child to obey the teachings of the Law. It is supposed to be a serious commitment before G-D that parents make for their child. They are responsible to teach the child the Jewish way of life.

I am certain that my parents, like most Jewish people, did not realize the seriousness of this event. Nevertheless, this was my first introduction to the religion of my forefathers. I was born a Jew, and the rite of circumcision was the external symbol binding me to Judaism.

## THE SOUND OF THUNDER: SUMMER 1954

I remember at the age of five playing catch with my neighborhood friend Bobby on a hot summer afternoon. We were enjoying each other's company when suddenly we heard the sound of thunder off in the distance. The sky had darkened, and a storm was brewing. Bobby perked his head up in fear.

"What's wrong, Bobby?" I asked.

"Did you hear that?" he replied, his blue eyes open wide with fear.

"It's only thunder," I laughed.

Another clap of thunder sounded. This time it was much louder. Bobby screamed so loudly it frightened me. He dropped the ball and began crying. "Mommy! Mommy!" he called as he ran quickly toward his house.

"Oh, come on, Bobby! Thunder can't hurt you," I shouted after him.

"Oh, yes it can!" he shouted back as he ran into the arms of his mother just outside his house. Another louder clap sounded, driving Bobby into hysteria.

"He thinks thunder can hurt you!" I yelled over to her.

She shouted back, "Thunder can't hurt you, but lightning can kill you. You better go into your house!"

Bobby and his mother went inside their home. I was left alone. I looked up at the darkened skies, wondering about the truth of what I was told. Suddenly, a flash of lightning lit the sky all around me. The loudest clap of thunder in the world seemed to shake the very ground I stood on.

I began to cry as I ran as fast as I could toward my house. The rain began to pour down as I slammed the door behind me. My fifteen-year-old sister, Fran, immediately came over to find out what was wrong. "The lightning can kill me," I cried as she stooped down, embracing me.

"No, no! Don't be afraid! It can't hurt you," she said emphatically.

"Yes, it can! Bobby's mom said it could kill me!" I yelled.

A flash of lightning filled the house, and a clap of thunder plunged me into major panic. Fran held me tighter and tried to comfort me. "Lightning can't hurt you, because G-D will protect you," she said softly.

I pulled away from her, puzzled—G-D? I had never heard that word before. "What is G-D?" I asked her.

"He's your friend. You can't see Him. He lives in a place called heaven, yet He is everywhere," she answered, smiling warmly and stroking my head tenderly. I remember looking around the room newly conscious of a presence I could not see. It was comforting, yet frightening at the same time. I totally forgot about the thunderstorm. All I could think about was this new person called G-D who was supposed to be near me wherever I went even though He was invisible.

Shortly thereafter I had a dream. I found myself walking on clouds as lighting and thunder surrounded me. I was frightened, but then the clouds began to part before me revealing a bright and golden circle of light in the distance. I felt as if I was being drawn closer toward the light as colorful beams began to emanate from its center. The colored rays of light came toward me and were all around me. They formed a pathway toward the light, which was almost blinding.

I felt tremendous peace and security as I continued to be drawn closer to the source of the light. The source had a pattern I would later recognize. It was shaped exactly like the golden light that surrounded the two tablets in Cecil B. DeMille's epic film *The Ten Commandments*, though I did not see the movie until years later! And then I heard the most beautiful and soothing voice. It seemed to surround me, yet it was also inside me as it said, "I am your friend. Don't be afraid. I will never hurt you."

I did not want to wake up from the dream. It was so real and comforting! I immediately tried to tell my mother what I had seen. "Mom, I saw G-D!"

She looked at me strangely. "You saw G-D?"

I answered her, "Yes, in my dream!"

She continued making me breakfast and commented, "That's nice!"

I told my father the same thing. He started laughing, "Really?" It seemed as if no one could appreciate what had so impacted me.

The next day in kindergarten class I tried to draw a picture of what I had seen in my dream. I used a yellow crayon and became very frustrated because I couldn't draw it better.

A little boy next to me asked what I was drawing.

"I'm drawing a picture of G-D," I told him.

"You can't draw a picture of G-D. No one can see Him," the boy said, laughing.

"Well, I saw G-D," I told the boy quietly.

Suddenly my classmate started shouting at me for all the class to hear. "You can't see G-D! He's invisible! Teacher, he said he saw G-D!"

I was embarrassed. I remember feeling all eyes on me. I began to cry.

"I did see G-D—in my dream!" I told the teacher tearfully.

She quieted the class down as she came over to me. I remember her taking the drawing from my desk and staring at it. She then looked at me with a puzzled expression. To this day I wonder how it affected her.

I am reminded often of this incident. I now realize I had seen the Lord G-D Almighty in my dream and was trying to draw a picture so I could show others His reality. I still have the drawing to this day and have included a picture of it in the photo section of this book. Little did I know, years later, that I would still be "drawing pictures" of G-D's reality, not with kindergarten crayons and construction paper, but rather on the canvas of motion picture film. Nothing could make a little five-year-old boy desire to communicate to others the reality of G-D unless G-D Himself planted that urge deep within.

G-D's plan for my life was made evident through a childhood dream. The Bible says that G-D chooses us before we are ever born. (See Ephesians 1:3–14.) I didn't realize then but what I had encountered was the Shekinah glory of the one true G-D of Israel.

## THE BEARER OF THE GLORY

Recently when I was in Israel on a tour, the Israeli tour guide began talking about how Jewish names have deeper meanings. I shared with him that my mother named me the Hebrew/Yiddish name, Wolf Meyer. The tour guide responded, "Wolf is a Yiddish name, but Meyer is Hebrew. It means in English, 'the bearer of the glory—or he who reveals the light!'"

The moment the words came out of his mouth, I was transported back to that childhood dream where I beheld the clouds parting to reveal the most beautiful golden light. I could sense the euphoria again as I could see in my mind's eye the beams of light radiating out from the source, enfolding me, engulfing me, and surrounding me. I remembered the unparalleled sense of peace as I was being drawn into the very source of the light itself.

What was it I beheld in my childhood dream? This dream was so significant that it placed within me a desire to know the one true G-D of Israel in the most intimate way.

What was that light? I am convinced that it was the Shekinah glory of G-D, which is the magnificent countenance of G-D in the form of light. It's the manifestation of the one true G-D of Israel hidden within a cloud of glory.

## "DO NOT BE AFRAID"

Many biblical scholars note that when Moses first had an encounter with the one true G-D of Israel, it was not G-D Himself but an angel (a messenger) of the Lord in the burning bush. Yet the Scriptures clearly indicate that the voice he heard was that of G-D Himself.

> The angel of the LORD appeared to him in a flame of fire from the midst of a bush.... When the LORD saw that he turned aside to see, [G-D] called to him from out of the midst of the bush and said, "Moses, Moses."
>
> And he said, "Here am I."
>
> He said, "Do not approach here. Remove your sandals from off your feet, for the place on which you are standing is holy ground." Moreover He said, "I am the [G-D] of your father, the [G-D] of Abraham, the [G-D] of Isaac, and the [G-D] of Jacob." And Moses hid his face, for he was afraid to look upon [G-D].
>
> —EXODUS 3:2, 4–6

Moses was not even in the full presence of the Shekinah glory but instead in the presence of the burning bush. Yet instead of sensing peace, he became afraid and hid his face.

When the children of Israel came out of Egypt, the one true G-D of Israel appeared to them in the cloud of His glory on Mount Sinai. Instead of sensing peace, they were in deep fear. When they heard the voice of G-D speaking to them, they begged Moses for G-D to stop letting them hear His voice. They wanted Moses to be the one who would meet with G-D and then tell them what He had to say.

Then on Mount Sinai the one true G-D of Israel appeared as the Shekinah glory in the midst of a cloud. Moses spoke as if face-to-face with Him. As Moses got to know Him better, there appeared to be a reverence he had for G-D but also a sense of security, peace, and euphoria.

Whenever the Shekinah glory of the one true G-D of Israel came and filled the holy of holies in the tabernacle and then in the holy temple in Jerusalem, the power of G-D was so awesome in His holiness that the priests couldn't stand up to minister until they became accustomed to being in His presence.

There was a notable difference between my first encounter with [G-D] in my dream as a five-year-old boy and that which I see recorded in the Bible concerning the fear others experienced. I believe that this is the message that I have been charged with sharing with you and others! In my childhood dream I was frightened of the lightning and thunder, but when the glory light of G-D was manifested, instead of fear I sensed overwhelming peace, comfort, and joy. G-D's voice was the most beautiful sound that echoed outside me but then resonated inside me. The words He spoke are the key message of *The Priestly Prayer of the Blessing.*

I heard Him say, "Do not be afraid. I am your friend and I will *never* hurt you."

Beholding the one true G-D of Israel in the form of His Shekinah glory and hearing His voice with those specific words impacted me and led me to become intimate with Him. They taught me that He is not just sitting on His distant throne; He is very near to me.

Years later, through the Priestly Prayer of the Blessing, my entire understanding of the reality and person of the one true G-D of Israel has been forever changed. My prayer is that what I am about to share with you in this book will also transform you and help you to walk in His supernatural favor and blessings.

I'm sure my mother had no idea about the fullness of meaning of my name. Did G-D impress upon her to name me Meyer? In this book I am acting as "the bearer of the glory—or he who reveals the light"! I believe that my life's message is now being disseminated to usher in the greatest end-time revival the world has ever experienced.

The Bible puts it this way concerning our divine destiny and purpose: "Just as He chose us in Him before the foundation of the world..." (Eph. 1:4). G-D's plan for my life, now revealed, would take years to begin to realize its full potential.

## REVEALING HIMSELF AGAIN

In light of that childhood dream I had a sense of G-D's reality and His presence. I would talk to Him continually as a friend. After the experience of being in His Shekinah glory, I wanted to find out more about who the one true G-D of Israel truly is.

My neighborhood in Linden, New Jersey, consisted of Jewish and Christian families living in peace together. None of my friends appeared to have had an experience like mine. We would talk about G-D, but only on the surface. I remember a group of us lying on the grass, gazing up at the stars on a hot summer night. The one thing we all agreed upon was that there had to be a Creator.

My mother, Pearl, was raised in an Orthodox Jewish home. My father, Charley, was raised by a wonderful, loving Jewish mother, but his dad claimed to be an atheist even though he was born Jewish. My father didn't appreciate religion. In his opinion they were after his money.

It was my mother who would begin to take me to the synagogue every *Shabbat* (Saturday). The reality of G-D's presence, which I experienced in my childhood dream, wasn't to be found in the synagogue I attended. Occasionally my mother would take me to Brooklyn, New York to visit my Orthodox grandparents on the high Jewish holy days, but even these lacked the power and majesty I experienced through that dream. Yet, just as G-D revealed Himself to me in a childhood dream, He would reveal Himself again, but this time on the screen of the Linden movie theater.

When I was eight years old, my mother took me to see the motion picture epic *The Ten Commandments*. I was riveted to the screen for the entire movie. I didn't even leave my seat during intermission to get more popcorn because I was afraid we would return late and miss a portion of the movie.

There was the one true G-D of Israel, bigger than life, talking to Moses from the burning bush. When Moses's staff transformed into a snake, I realized that the G-D of Israel was a G-D of signs, wonders, and miracles. G-D manifested Himself as the judge of the unrighteous as the ten plagues fell upon the Egyptian nation. I marveled at the pillar of fire as it held back the great armies of Pharaoh and as the Red Sea dramatically parted, allowing the children of Israel to walk to the other side on completely dry ground. I cheered as the sea closed on the pursuing Egyptian army, destroying the enemies of Israel.

My heart pounded within me with an unexplainable fear and wonder as I watched Moses confronting the G-D of Israel face-to-face on Mount Sinai. I truly sensed the reality of G-D's presence again as His fingers carved the Ten Commandments on stone. There I was in a movie theater, yet I felt the presence of G-D all around me. It was the same feeling I experienced in my childhood dream. The voice of G-D in the movie was just like the voice I heard in my dream. Even the magnificent countenance of G-D in the form of light—the Shekinah glory—was similar to His appearance in my dream. I could feel my heart beating quickly and hard.

Suddenly I remembered what G-D had told me in the dream, "Do not be afraid. I am your friend, and I will never hurt you."

I thought, "This G-D who placed plagues upon the Egyptians, parted the Red Sea, and destroyed the Egyptian army is *my* friend?"

An immense supernatural peace seemed to flood my being. Then I beheld the children of Israel rejecting G-D in the valley of Mount Sinai, thinking Moses was not coming back. They partied and worshipped the golden calf.

No preacher could have ever delivered a sermon as powerful as what I witnessed with my entire being in that movie theater. The reality of G-D had overtaken me. Not only was my G-D the One who performed miracles, but He was also a G-D of judgment. I gazed in awe as He opened the earth to swallow those who refused to repent of worshipping the golden calf as if this idol was the one true G-D of Israel.

The sense of G-D's awe went home with me from the movie theater. Weeks later at the synagogue I heard the rabbi talking about the movie. He tried to make apologies for the Torah, which describes the parting of the Red Sea in the same miraculous manner as the film.

Dressed in his black religious robe of authority, he addressed the congregation, "The Torah is full of wonderful stories with great moral teachings. Some of the events are based on true events, others are based on oral tales, later embellished by the writer. Of course, we don't take these stories literally."

I felt like a deflated balloon as the rabbi spoke. Could it be that what gave me such hope and joy is nothing but a story?

The rabbi continued, "I once heard an Israeli scientist describe a theory of how the Red Sea could have parted. It is reported that once every thousand years a great mystery of science prevails in that area of the Middle East. The Red Sea dries up and parts become low enough to walk over. So, the actual event was something quite possible and commonplace, but the timing of this natural scientific phenomenon made it a miracle."

As the rabbi smiled at the wisdom he imparted, I was deeply troubled. He might have explained away the parting of the Red Sea, but how did this prevent Pharaoh's armies from pursuing the children of Israel with their chariots? The ground would have been hard and dry! The Torah lesson I had heard said that they all were destroyed as the water came down upon them.

When the service was dismissed, everyone was invited into the synagogue's gymnasium to partake of Oneg Shabbat (refreshments to enhance the Sabbath joy). As the people in the congregation socialized, I wandered back into the empty sanctuary. I looked toward the altar where the ark stood that contained the Torah scrolls.

I longed to see the one true G-D of Israel as He appeared to me in my dream. I wanted to see Him like He appeared to Moses in the motion picture *The Ten Commandments*. I called out, "Oh G-D, where are You? Please show Yourself to me!"

There was nothing but silence. Tears began streaming down my face. I cried out to Him again, "G-D, please show Yourself—I know You can!" I wanted to see Him appear right before me. The fact that He didn't only made me have more resolve to see Him again. The experience of the dream and then the movie planted a seed deep within me.

Another motion picture that had great impact upon me was *Ben-Hur*. Again, it was my mother who took me to the theater to see it. I instantly became engrossed in the scope of this epic picture. The biblical story line pictured the person of *Yeshua* (Jesus) as the Messiah in a compassionate but mysterious way. We never saw His face, but His presence was revealed in brief glimpses throughout the story.

I was deeply moved as Yeshua gave the meek and thirsty main character, played by Charlton Heston, a drink of water. You could see only the hand of Jesus, but the glow on the face of Charlton Heston as he looked into the eyes of Yeshua conveyed the majesty of the Messiah's presence.

Yet nothing could have prepared me for the deeply moving scenes of the final hours of Yeshua. The passion of the cross overtook me as I witnessed a beaten form of a man carrying His cross. I was moved to tears as Charlton Heston carried the cross for Yeshua.

The dramatic climax took my breath away as I silently watched Yeshua agonizing on the cross with nails in His hands and feet. Tears began to roll down my cheeks as I asked myself, "Why did they have to kill this innocent, gentle man?"

The glorious conclusion of the movie raptured me into another world; a sense of the reality of G-D's presence began to fill my being. It all seemed so real as the sky darkened and the lightning flashed and the thunder rolled. Before my eyes the lepers were healed, and somehow I knew that I had met a great man of G-D in Yeshua.

After the movie was over, I asked my mother if Yeshua was a real person. I wanted Him to be real. I wanted the story to be true, but she turned and said, "No, it was just a story."

The reality of the one true G-D of Israel had once more overtaken me through the viewing of a motion picture. Words alone couldn't convey the powerful truth of G-D's holy words. I was reminded of my own frustration of trying to tell my mom and dad about the dream I had of seeing G-D. I responded by trying to draw a picture of G-D in my kindergarten class depicting the image of how He appeared to me in the form of the Shekinah glory. It had been my desire to convey the awesome vision I witnessed in my dream of the one true G-D of Israel.

The movie screen had a way of transcending reality unlike any other medium. Through the creative use of the camera, lighting, sound, and editing, motion pictures have a way of transporting us right into the very screen and the story being portrayed. The motion picture can affect the intellect, the emotion, and the very spirit of humanity.

As an eight-year-old in the theater that night, I realized that G-D can use the motion picture as a means to speak to the masses, just as He used a burning bush to speak to Moses. I decided that I wanted to become a filmmaker and produce movies that say what G-D would have me say.

I began reading every book from the library concerning the art of motion picture production. By the time I reached twelve years old, I began to say a nightly prayer to G-D. I wrote on a piece of paper a prayer that I would repeat every night for one year: "Oh G-D, whoever You are, I ask that You make me a great producer, director, writer, cameraman, and editor, and I will make films that say only what You want me to say." (I have included a photo of this prayer in the photo section.)

I didn't even know who G-D really was, nor did I understand how I would be able to hear His instructions. All I wanted was to be used by Him to bless others. This quest to know the one true G-D of Israel remained with me throughout my life.

After graduating high school in 1967, I attended the School of Visual Arts in New York City to study the art of motion pictures. I was taught by professionals who actually worked in the film industry as producers, directors, cinematographers, screenwriters, and motion picture film editors.

From 1970 through 1976 I worked on Madison Avenue as an award-winning writer, producer, film director/cinematographer, and motion picture editor. Then from 1978 through 1986 I worked for the Christian Broadcasting Network (CBN) in Virginia Beach, Virginia.

Imagine a Jewish boy from Brooklyn, New York, producing two series of animated Bible stories for children, *SuperBook* and *Flying House*, for a Christian TV network!

The highlight of my time at CBN was producing and directing the highest-rated religious TV special of all time, *Don't Ask Me, Ask God*. The most impressive part is that when the host of the program, Pat Robertson, offered a prayer of salvation, more than 114,000 letters came flooding into CBN. These were individuals, even entire families, who testified that they had bowed their heads and received Yeshua as their Messiah.

After leaving CBN, I served as the president of Dr. Jerry Falwell's Liberty Broadcasting Network in Lynchburg, Virginia, from 1986 through 2003. I was also the executive producer of Jerry Falwell's *Old Time Gospel Hour* weekly TV program, and I oversaw the production of programs for children, teens, and the family, including *Act It Out, Over the Hill Gang,* and *Backstage With Gary McSpadden*.

I began my own 501c3 ministry, New Day Pictures International Inc., in 1991 and produced a series of award-winning filmed documentaries on revival, *Go Inside the Toronto Blessing, Go Inside the Smithton Outpouring,* and *The Brownsville Revival*. While filming these documentaries, I was profoundly impacted, and I received a passion to see people walk in intimacy with the one true G-D of Israel and experience G-D's power to walk in the supernatural.

At the time of writing this book, I serve as vice president of Sid Roth's *It's Supernatural!* and Messianic Vision Inc., where I oversee the production of TV programs and the filming of many of the dramatic film segments that bring to life the testimonies of people who have experienced the supernatural of the one true G-D of Israel.

It's been a long journey to fully understand the significance of my childhood dream and encounter with the one true G-D of Israel in the form of the Shekinah glory. As a little boy I wanted to tell everyone about Him, yet nobody would listen to me. So I did the next best thing. I tried to draw a picture in kindergarten in order to share what I had seen in my dream. Today I am using motion pictures and television to share the revelation of the one true G-D. The saying goes, "A picture is worth a thousand words!" It's as if G-D Himself placed this calling, purpose, and destiny into my being, even before I fully understood who He was (Eph. 1:4–5).

## KEYS TO THE BLESSING

One encounter with the one true G-D of Israel can change the total direction of our lives!

## STUDY QUESTIONS

What was the dream Warren had concerning his meeting with the one true G-D of Israel?

_____

_____

_____

How did people in the Bible react when they were in the presence of angels (messengers of the Most High G-D of Israel) or when G-D's Shekinah glory was revealed?

_____

_____

_____

What does Warren say is the key message that the one true G-D of Israel spoke to him in his childhood dream?

_____

_____

_____

What significance do the words G-D uttered to Warren in his dream mean for you?

_____

_____

_____

What was it in the motion picture *The Ten Commandments* that affected Warren when he was an eight-year-old?

_____

_____

_____

What was Warren's reaction when his rabbi downplayed the supernatural event of the parting of the Red Sea?

_____

_____

_____

How did the movie *Ben-Hur* affect Warren?

_____

_____

_____

Can you see how G-D has called each of us to a God-given destiny and purpose before the foundations of the world? (See Ephesians 1:4–5.) What do you think G-D has called you to do?

_____

_____

_____

# SECTION II:
# THE FOUNDATION FOR UNDERSTANDING THE PRAYER

## Chapter 3

# HOW TO ACCESS THE FULL IMPARTATION

REMEMBER, THIS JOURNEY began when my friend Rick Amato told me about the discovery of an artifact containing the ancient Priestly Prayer of the Blessing and the powerful experience he had when this prayer was prayed over him. In chapter 1 we investigated several questions that were troubling me concerning why Rick had been so affected by the prayer and found that they were not a factor. It wasn't because he was so near the place of discovery. Nor was there a special portal to the heavens. Neither was it in the power of the amulet itself.

In my continuing search for why Rick had been so affected by the Priestly Prayer of the Blessing, the following questions remained.

+ Why was the high priest Aaron the one to proclaim it daily over the children of Israel instead of Moses?

+ What does it mean that the one true G-D of Israel placed His name on the children of Israel?

+ What about the fact that the Priestly Prayer of the Blessing was said in Hebrew and not English?

+ Where does the power come from that affected Rick?

## IT'S TIME TO GO DEEPER

Remember, the Priestly Prayer of the Blessing is found in the Book of Numbers.

The LORD bless you and keep you; the LORD make His face to shine upon you, and be gracious unto you; the LORD lift His countenance upon you, and give you peace.

—NUMBERS 6:24–26

This prayer is amazing in light of the fact that it is the only prayer in the entire Bible that was written by the one true G-D of Israel. The words to this blessing are a beautiful expression of G-D's love toward us. Yet we must understand that there are various degrees of benefit we receive from anything written in the Bible. In Judaism there are several different levels of understanding G-D's Word: *peshat, remez, derash,* and *sod.*

*Peshat* is understanding the surface or literal meaning. *Remez* deals with a deeper truth that the text is hinting at or pointing to. *Derash* is an elucidation of the text. *Sod* is the secret or hidden meaning buried in the nuances of the Hebrew letters and words.[1]

In a similar way, I believe there are deeper levels of blessing and understanding available to us, and I've identified seven of them. One level of benefit comes from just reading the Word of G-D. A second level by meditating on the Word. Still a greater portion of blessing comes when we begin studying its deeper meaning and connection on how the verses relate to other passages in the Bible. An even deeper level occurs when we study the Hebrew or Greek meaning of the words themselves. Often the English translators had to decide what definition each word conveys in order to include the essence of what they concurred was the correct meaning.

The fifth level is transformation as it manifests as the Word of G-D affecting our very thinking. A sixth and even deeper impact comes from G-D Himself as His Holy Spirit writes the meaning upon our hearts. But the seventh and greatest impartation comes when G-D manifests Himself—His very person—to us, dwells within us and upon us, and flows out from us to others. The result is a tangible change in our minds, hearts, souls, and circumstances. As a consequence we obtain supernatural breakthroughs!

Most believers are either not cognizant that deeper levels exist or they have never been challenged to pursue such. They are unaware of the great blessings that ensue. When we receive the fullness of impartation, which G-D Himself intended to be experienced, there is no limit to what is possible!

As you continue reading this book you will be taken through each of the seven levels until you begin to receive the fullness of blessings that G-D has in store for you just as the children of Israel and those in the early church experienced.

## ISRAEL'S HIGH PRIESTS

There is something important to remember. The verse immediately following the Priestly Prayer of the Blessing gives us an important key as to why Israel received the outpouring of the supernatural that G-D intended.

> They will put My name upon the children of Israel, and I will bless them.
>
> —NUMBERS 6:27

As I mulled over the questions that still remained about Rick Amato's experience, it became apparent that the hidden key in verse 27 was of a greater significance than I had comprehended. Why did G-D want the high priest to be the only one to proclaim this prayer of blessing every day over the children of Israel instead of Moses?

Initially it was Moses himself who acted as an intercessor on behalf of the children of Israel and the Most High G-D. He would meet with the one true G-D of Israel who came in the form of the Shekinah glory first on Mount Sinai and then within the temporary dwelling place called the "tent of the meeting." When Moses spent time in the presence of the Shekinah glory, his face would begin to display that glory. When he came back to the people to share what G-D had told him, the children of Israel begged Moses to put a veil on his face because they were frightened of the reflection of G-D's glory that shone on Moses's face.

Once the tabernacle in the wilderness was constructed, G-D descended into the innermost tent called the "holy of holies" in the form of the Shekinah glory. Moses could not enter in to meet with G-D as he had done before. No one could enter into the holy of holies except the high priest of Israel once a year on the Hebrew feast of Yom Kippur (the Day of Atonement) to bring a sacrifice for the atonement of the nation of Israel.

One of the main reasons that only the high priest could administer the Priestly Prayer of the Blessing is that he was the agent who could dispense a supernatural impartation of a portion of the Shekinah glory onto the children of Israel—a portion that he received through being the only one able to enter into the holy of holies. I am proposing that just as Moses was powerfully affected by being in the Shekinah glory of the Most High G-D, so too was the high priest Aaron.

The high priest was an intermediary between the children of Israel and the one true G-D of Israel. Why was an intermediary needed? Under the old covenant the high priest was the only one allowed to go into the holy of holies to meet with YHWH once a year on the Day of Atonement.

Every morning the high priest (and the priests who served under him) had to be set apart (made holy) before they could administer their priestly functions and service unto G-D as prescribed in the Torah. Each had to offer up for themselves blood sacrifices (such as sin and trespass offerings) in order to deal with their personal sins and obtain forgiveness. Then they had to wash themselves with the water from the bronze laver. Both blood and holy water were applied to them. Not only must this blood and holy water be applied to them, but also these two elements had to be applied to all the vessels of the tabernacle to make them holy for service unto G-D. The priests had to wear certain vestments (clothing) designed by G-D Himself.

Every day all of the priests, including Aaron the high priest, would have set themselves apart to be holy. In Exodus 29 we read what was required by G-D.

+ The sacrifice of an unblemished bullock and two unblemished rams—the shedding of blood to atone for their own sins—representing inward cleansing

+ Unleavened bread from the altar of showbread—representing communion with G-D

+ Washing of holy water from the bronze laver—representing outward cleansing

+ Wearing special priestly garments designed by G-D Himself—visually displaying their authority to represent G-D

+ The anointing had to be poured over their heads

+ Burnt offerings needed to be made

+ A consecration offering, the application of the blood to the tip of the right ear, right thumb, and big toe of right foot

+ A wave offering would then be consummated

Only the Levitical priests could enter the tabernacle; the people of Israel had to stay far away from the outer walls. Before the full tabernacle was erected, G-D Himself wanted the children of Israel to see that Moses truly met with Him. G-D wanted them to know He was there for them, to watch over, protect, and bless them.

Before G-D established the tabernacle and the old covenant priesthood after the order of Aaron, the children of Israel were told by Moses according to G-D's instructions to prepare themselves by washing their clothing and abstaining from sexual relations for three days. On that day they stood far off from the temporary "tent of meeting" pitched by Moses. G-D's Shekinah glory descended inside this temporary dwelling place. Moses would enter to meet with G-D on behalf of the children of Israel as their intermediary. The people witnessed the supernatural cloud by day and the pillar of fire by night, which appeared from heaven over the place where the Shekinah glory would reside.

The point I am making is that there was always an intercessor needed in the old covenant. At first it was Moses who would meet with the one true G-D on behalf of the children of Israel. Then once the tabernacle in the wilderness was constructed as commanded by G-D Himself, and then the holy temple, only the high priest could meet directly with G-D in the holy of holies once a year as a representative of the people.

Most of my brethren today, the Jewish people, don't understand that no one in Israel could directly access the presence of the one true G-D apart from an intercessor. There was a priest, but not just any priest, that could pronounce the Priestly Prayer of the Blessing over the children of Israel. It was only the high priest who would come out of the tabernacle (and later the holy temple in Jerusalem) and meet with the people each day standing before them. In the *Tanakh* (Old Testament) other less significant functions were often administered by Levitical priests, such as the administration of sacrifices, anointing with oil, and carrying out the daily priestly duties of the sacrificial system.

In other instances the heads of the twelve tribes of Israel would stand in the gap and administer certain ministry functions on behalf of the people within each tribe. There were many layers between the people of G-D and access to the awesome presence of G-D who made Himself manifest in the form of the Shekinah glory.

Following the practices of the patriarchs of Israel, the father of each Jewish family was encouraged by the rabbis to administer blessings by laying his hand on the heads of his children. The foundation of laying on of hands in the new covenant is based on that same foundation laid out in the old covenant. In the church today it is the "elders of the church" who are encouraged to lay hands upon the sick and anoint them with oil when they pray for their healing. (See 1 Timothy 4:14; James 5:14.)

As I already stated, the high priest was the only one who could administer the Priestly Prayer of the Blessing. Not even Moses, who had met with G-D in the glory cloud and talked directly with Him as if face-to-face (Exod. 33:11), could pronounce this blessing over the people.

In modern times, during Passover there will be events in Israel by the Western Wall (the *Kotel*) where rabbis with the name Cohen will pronounce the Priestly Prayer of the Blessing over the Jewish people who gather there. The rabbinical authorities believe that those with the name Cohen could be descendants of the Levitical priests, which in Hebrew are called *kohen* or plural *kohanim*. But honestly the bloodline ancestry of those with the name Cohen cannot truly be established.

As beautiful as this ceremony is, the fullness of the supernatural power of this blessing is not anything like it was when the high priest Aaron administered it over the children of Israel every day. Again, one of the main reasons is that the high priest was the only person able to enter into the holy of holies to meet directly with the one true G-D of Israel.

Please understand, as with any portion of the Word of G-D, this divine prayer of blessing is unique and will bless you in proportion to whatever level you engage with it. Here are the seven levels again:

1. Reading the Word of G-D.

2. Meditating on the Word.

3. Studying its deeper meaning and making a connection on how the verses relate to other passages throughout the Bible.

4. Studying the Hebrew or Greek meaning of the words themselves.

5. Allowing the Word of G-D to affect your very thinking. In Scripture, this is referred to as "the washing with water through the word [of G-D]" (Eph. 5:26, NIV).

6. Reaching a deeper impact as a result of an impartation from G-D Himself as His Holy Spirit writes the meaning upon your heart.

7. The greatest impartation comes when G-D manifests Himself—His very person—to us and dwells within us and upon us and flows out from us to others! The result is a tangible change in our circumstances, and as a consequence we obtain supernatural breakthroughs to fulfill our calling, destiny, and purpose while on planet Earth.

I believe G-D has revealed to me the way in which you and I can receive the same supernatural fullness that the children of Israel received as the high priest Aaron administered the divine prayer over them in the wilderness every day for forty years!

## OUR HIGH PRIEST

Only after the high priest of Israel completed the cleansing and anointing process would he exit the tabernacle and come before the children of Israel who were assembled outside every morning. No hands of the high priest were ever laid upon them.

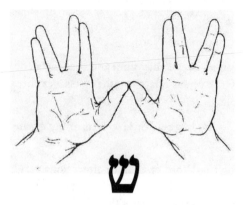

While pronouncing this blessing, Aaron extended his hands toward the people, spreading his fingers apart and placing his thumbs together to represent the Hebrew letter *shin*, an emblem for *El Shaddai*. This represented G-D Almighty. (The Hebrew word *dai* means "to shed forth, to pour out, or to heap benefits.")

Through the high priest of Israel, a little portion of the actual Shekinah glory (the manifest presence of the one true G-D of Israel) was "shed forth or poured out" upon the children of Israel in a supernatural way!

The children of Israel did not have the Ruach HaKodesh (Holy Spirit) residing *within* them. The manifestation of the Holy Spirit within only occurred as a result of Yeshua's promise that it would be far better when He was gone because they would receive the indwelt Holy Spirit.

> I will pray the Father, and He will give you another Counselor, that He may be with you forever: the Spirit of truth, whom the world cannot receive, for it does not see Him, neither does it know Him. But you know Him, for He lives with you, and will be in you.
>
> —JOHN 14:16–17

The first promise as a result of the new covenant is that all believers who accept by faith Yeshua (Jesus) as their Messiah would have the Holy Spirit *within* them.

> Then I will sprinkle clean water upon you, and you shall be clean. From all your filthiness and from all your idols, I will cleanse you.

> Also, I will give you a new heart, and a new spirit [a new nature]
> I will put within you. And I will take away the stony heart out of
> your flesh, and I will give you a heart of flesh. I will put My Spirit
> [Holy Spirit] within you and cause you to walk in My statutes,
> and you will keep My judgments and do them.
> —EZEKIEL 36:25–27

The children of Israel also didn't have the Holy Spirit *upon* them.
Under the old covenant the Holy Spirit was only placed upon certain men such as prophets, kings, and priests. On one occasion, the
Holy Spirit came upon a donkey ridden by the prophet Balaam,
causing the donkey to speak and forbid the madness of the prophet
(Num. 22:28).

But the second promise as a result of the new covenant was that all
believers—not just some special appointed people such as prophets,
kings, and priests—would one day also have the Holy Spirit placed
*upon* them, so they too could be witnesses and demonstrate G-D's
kingdom on earth.

> And it shall come to pass afterward, that I will pour out my spirit
> *upon all flesh*; and your sons and your daughters shall prophesy,
> your old men shall dream dreams, your young men shall see
> visions: And also upon the servants and upon the handmaids in
> those days will I pour out my spirit.
> —JOEL 2:28–29, KJV

G-D gave to Moses the *Torah* (G-D's written precepts, commandments, and instruction) to guide the children of Israel in the covenant that He had forged with them. The rabbis have deduced to the
best of their corporate ability that there are 613 different commandments. These were to be followed in "blind obedience"—no questions
asked! If a person sinned against G-D, His grace was available for
forgiveness through the sacrificial system of atonement and trespass
offerings, which included the shedding of the blood of *kosher* (clean,
unblemished) animals.

Truthfully none of us could ever live up to such a high calling,
especially without the Holy Spirit upon us or within us, except for
the provision of grace, which in the old covenant was given through
the shedding of the blood of unblemished animals. This foundational

truth that a sacrifice was needed to atone for our sins is also the main foundational truth contained in the new covenant.

> For the life of the flesh is in the blood, and I have given it to you on the altar to make atonement for your lives; for it is the blood that makes atonement for the soul.
>
> —LEVITICUS 17:11

My point is that G-D *did* give the children of Israel something special, and He did not leave them without supernatural help. Through this Priestly Prayer of the Blessing pronounced by the high priest over them every day, G-D would be placing His very person (in the form of a portion of the Shekinah glory) upon them in a supernatural way. My contention is that this was a different manifestation than what occurs when one receives Yeshua as Messiah and Lord and when Ruach HaKodesh (Holy Spirit) comes to reside within (Ezek. 11:19; 36:26–27) and the manifestation that occurs when the Holy Spirit comes upon us (Joel 2:28–29).

What does occur through the impartation of this divine prayer is what happened to the children of Israel for forty years while they were in the wilderness—supernatural provision, supernatural health, angelic protection, and prosperity! Even their shoes and clothes never wore out.

These miracles happened to them as a result of the proclamation of the Priestly Prayer of the Blessing over them by the high priest every day. Through the pronouncement of this divine prayer in the manner prescribed through G-D Himself, a portion of the Shekinah glory (the very person of G-D the Father) was placed upon them.

What if this is possible for us to have today? I believe as you read this book, you will discover that G-D wants us to experience this today. What I am about to share with you is how you can begin to walk in divine intimacy with the one true G-D of Israel, your heavenly Father, and it begins with an understanding of the Shekinah glory.

Are you ready to understand more?

## KEYS TO THE BLESSING

Only the high priest could pronounce the Priestly Prayer of the Blessing over the children of Israel by lifting his hands and placing his fingers in a way to represent the name of G-D.

## STUDY QUESTIONS

Why was it that the high priest was the only one who could pronounce the divine prayer over the children of Israel?

_____

_____

_____

What did the high priest, after the order of Aaron, have to do before he could minister in the holy of holies and later in the holy temple in Jerusalem?

_____

_____

_____

When the high priest of Israel held both hands up with his fingers in the form of the Hebrew letter *shin*, what did this signify and what did the children of Israel receive upon them?

_____

_____

_____

What different manifestation can we as believers in Yeshua receive that is different than that of receiving the Holy Spirit within and then upon us?

_____

_____

_____

## PRAYER

*Father G-D, I come before You and ask that You continue to help me grasp this teaching and let the truth of this revelation affect not only my intellect—my mind—but I pray You write it upon my heart so I will receive all You have intended for me to experience! I pray this in the name of Yeshua (Jesus).*

## Chapter 4

# WHAT IS THE SHEKINAH GLORY?

TODAY I HEAR many talking about the glory as if it's the same thing as the Ruach HaKodesh (Holy Spirit). You will hear some say, "The Holy Spirit came as the glory upon us and many were saved, delivered, and healed!"

Then you will also hear some say things such as, "The glory of G-D came into the room and charged the atmosphere. There was a tangible glory cloud. People were healed and set free in a dramatic way like we had never seen before. There was no laying on of hands. People were receiving miracles and healing all over the room."

What is the glory? Is there a difference between the Holy Spirit and the glory?

In the *Tanakh* (Old Testament) we read about the glory of G-D coming down from heaven and resting on top of Mount Sinai.

> Moses went up to the mountain, and the cloud covered the mountain. The glory of the LORD rested on Mount Sinai, and the cloud covered it for six days. And on the seventh day He called to Moses *from* the midst of the cloud. Now the appearance of the glory of the LORD was like a consuming fire on the top of the mountain to the eyes of the children of Israel.
>
> —EXODUS 24:15–17

In other references we read that the glory of G-D entered the temporary dwelling place Moses built called the "tent of meeting" and later into the holy of holies in the tabernacle built by Moses, as well as in the first holy temple built later by Solomon and the second holy temple built under the leadership of Ezra and Nehemiah. (Herod merely reconstructed the second temple.)

> Then the cloud covered the tent of meeting, and the glory of the LORD filled the tabernacle. Moses was not able to enter into the

tent of meeting because the cloud settled on it, and the glory of
the LORD filled the tabernacle.

—EXODUS 40:34–35

The house, the house of the LORD, was filled with a cloud. And
the priests were not able to stand in order to serve because of the
cloud, for the glory of the LORD filled the house of [G-D].

—2 CHRONICLES 5:13–14

## WHAT EXACTLY IS THE SHEKINAH GLORY?

It couldn't have been the Holy Spirit, because the Holy Spirit would
fall upon certain prophets, priests, and kings. The Holy Spirit wasn't
contained to being just in the holy of holies. It wasn't Yeshua (Jesus)
because Yeshua had not yet been born of a virgin as the only begotten
Son of the G-D of Israel.

We've discussed that when it came to the tabernacle and the holy
temple, there was a separation between the children of Israel and the
glory that abode in the holy of holies. The high priest of Israel could
enter only once a year on *Yom Kippur* (the Day of Atonement) into
the holy of holies to offer the atonement sacrifice for the nation of
Israel as their intercessor. Moses went alone into the cloud of G-D's
glory on Mount Sinai.

A key to understanding the glory is given in Moses's encounter
with the G-D of Israel when he built the temporary tent of meeting,
a place for the Shekinah glory to abide until the full tabernacle
could be constructed. It was in the cloud of G-D's glory that Moses
beseeched G-D in the following verse.

Then Moses said, "I pray, show me Your glory."

—EXODUS 33:18

Moses stood in the cloud of G-D's glory. From all accounts, the
cloud was a covering masking the bright light of G-D's Shekinah
glory. Moses was saying that he wanted to get beyond the cloud itself
and go further inside to see clearly the fullness of the light of G-D's
glory. But the one true G-D of Israel identified the source of the light
that Moses was beholding.

Then [G-D] said, "I will make all My goodness pass before you,
and I will proclaim the name of the LORD before you. I will be

gracious to whom I will be gracious and will show mercy on whom I will show mercy." He said, "You cannot see *My face*, for no man can see Me and live."

—Exodus 33:19–20

It was the one true G-D of Israel who told Moses what the glory was—it was His face. The glory light was emitted from the very source, the very *face* of G-D the Father.

Let me submit to you that the glory is not a thing, but the glory is a person—the person of the one true G-D, the heavenly Father. Whenever Moses entered into the glory cloud, the reflection of G-D's glory would come upon Moses's face.

When Moses came down from Mount Sinai with the two tablets of testimony in the hands of Moses, when he came down from the mountain, Moses did not know that the skin of his face shone while he talked with Him. So when Aaron and all the children of Israel saw Moses, amazingly, the skin of his face shone, and they were afraid to come near him.

—Exodus 34:29–30

It is written that Moses had to place a veil upon his face in order for the children of Israel to not be afraid to approach Moses as he imparted the word given to him by G-D. In the Book of Revelation we read of the effect the glory of G-D has upon Yeshua since He is seated on the throne of mercy (the heavenly mercy seat) at the right hand of the heavenly Father.

Then I turned to see the voice that spoke with me. And when I turned, I saw seven golden candlesticks, and in the midst of the seven candlesticks was *one like a Son of Man, clothed with a garment down to the feet and with a golden sash wrapped around the chest. The hair on His head was white like wool, as white as snow. His eyes were like a flame of fire.* His feet were like fine brass, as if refined in a furnace, and His voice as the sound of many waters. He had in His right hand seven stars, out of His mouth went a sharp two-edged sword. His appearance was like the sun shining brightly. When I saw Him, I fell at His feet as though I were dead. Then He laid His right hand on me, saying to me, "Do not be afraid. I am the First and the Last. I am He who lives, though

I was dead. Look! I am alive forevermore. Amen. And I have the
keys of Hades and of Death."
—REVELATION 1:12–18

Again I stress to you that when Aaron the high priest of Israel
pronounced the Priestly Prayer of the Blessing upon the children
of Israel while holding both of his hands up toward the people, he
would spread his fingers and keep his thumbs together, to represent
the Hebrew letter *shin*, an emblem for El Shaddai (meaning G-D
Almighty), and something supernatural happened! A little portion
of the actual Shekinah glory (the presence of the one true G-D of
Israel) was "shed forth or poured out" upon the children of Israel!

Rabbinical literature refers to this as *nesiat kapayim*, the "lifting
of the hands." Jewish tradition states that the divine presence would
shine through the fingers of the high priest as he blessed the people,
and no one was allowed to look at this out of respect for G-D. This
appears to support the claim that a portion of the Shekinah glory
would pass through the window of the high priest's hands and come
onto the children of Israel.

Could it be that the hands of the high priest also were likened to
the wings of the cherubim, which were positioned over the ark of the
covenant's mercy seat where the Shekinah rested? The children of
Israel were to bow their heads, just as the cherubim on the ark were
fashioned as having their heads bowed in reverence.

## Hollywood and the Shekinah Glory

The famous TV and film personality Leonard Nimoy, who
played Spock in the TV series *Star Trek*, shares how he bor-
rowed the Vulcan salutation and the raising of his hand from
his Jewish upbringing.

Leonard Nimoy said in an interview, "So I'm with my father,
my grandfather, and my brother sitting in the bench seats....
Five or six guys get up on...the stage facing the congregation
and they get their *talit* [prayer shawls] over their heads, and
they start this chanting."[1] He shared that his father told him
not to look up. Everyone in the congregation covered their
eyes with their hands, and their talitot were over their heads.

Leonard said he sensed something powerful and decided to peek. He saw the rabbi's hands making the form of the Hebrew letter *shin*, an emblem for *shaddai*.

Leonard said it was much later before he found out why he wasn't supposed to look at the rabbi with his hands in the form of the *shin* while he pronounced the divine prayer. An Orthodox rabbi told him that during the benediction, the Shekinah comes into the sanctuary to bless the congregation. "You don't want to see that because it's so powerful...we could get seriously injured or it could be fatal. So that's why you protect yourself by hiding your eyes."[2]

Leonard later adapted the hand gesture into the greeting that his character Spock would give on *Star Trek* as the Vulcan salute with the words, "Live long and prosper!" These words are part of the actual Hebrew meaning of the Priestly Prayer of the Blessing.

The movie produced by Steven Spielberg *Raiders of the Lost Ark* centers on a story line that the ark of the covenant held supernatural power concerning the G-D of the Hebrews. In the climactic scene the Nazis had taken possession of the ark. Indiana Jones, along with the leading lady, Marion, were captured and tied to a stake while a Nazi dressed as the Jewish high priest began to invoke the G-D of Israel in the Hebrew language to manifest His glory. The powerful scene includes Hollywood special effects simulating the Shekinah glory beginning to manifest from within the ark as the cover is removed. Indiana Jones yells to the leading lady, "Marion, don't look at it—shut your eyes, Marion, no matter what happens!" The movie depicts that all the Nazis who gazed upon the Shekinah glory were destroyed—even burned to a crisp.

## YESHUA AND THE GLORY

In New Testament writings we also see evidence of the glory not being a thing but actually being the very person of the Most High G-D. The account of Yeshua on the Mount of Transfiguration speaks powerfully to this point.

> After six days Jesus took Peter, James, and John his brother and brought them up to a high mountain alone, and was transfigured before them. His face shone as the sun, and His garments became white as the light.
>
> —MATTHEW 17:1–2

Right here we have a clue to the fact that it was the Shekinah glory that Yeshua was being affected by as he was immersed in the glory light of G-D in full view of the disciples. This same sort of sign and wonder occurred when Moses was in the midst of the Shekinah glory on Mount Sinai.

> Suddenly Moses and Elijah appeared to them, talking with Him. Then Peter said to [Yeshua], "Lord, it is good for us to be here. If You wish, let us make three tabernacles here: one for You, one for Moses, and one for Elijah." While he was still speaking, suddenly a bright cloud overshadowed them, and a voice from the cloud said, "This is My beloved Son, with whom I am well pleased. Listen to Him."
>
> —MATTHEW 17:3–5

Note that it was a bright cloud that overshadowed them. Moses had stood numbers of times in the midst of the bright cloud of the Shekinah glory. Here were Peter, James, and John now standing in the midst of the cloud and what the Scriptures clearly indicate in verse 5 is a key to what the glory actually is.

> …a voice from the cloud said, "This is My beloved Son, with whom I am well pleased. Listen to Him."
>
> —MATTHEW 17:5

The one true G-D of Israel Himself, the heavenly Father, was in that cloud of glory and spoke to them about Yeshua being His only begotten Son. This was a key moment for the disciples to witness. They now knew that Yeshua was more than another great prophet as Moses and Elijah were regarded, but He was the only begotten Son of G-D.

> When the disciples heard this, they fell on their faces and were filled with awe.
>
> —MATTHEW 17:6

Here we see the awesome power of the presence of the Most High G-D of Israel, the heavenly Father, in the midst of the Shekinah glory. I have already shared with you that when the Shekinah glory came and filled the temple that Solomon built, the priests couldn't stand to minister. They were overcome!

> And when the priests came out of the holy place, the cloud filled the house of the LORD, so that the priests could not continue to minister because of the cloud, for the glory of the LORD filled the house of the LORD.
>
> —I KINGS 8:10–11

Yeshua had to reassure the disciples that they had the privilege of being witnesses to the appearance of the one true G-D of Israel, the heavenly Father, in the midst of the Shekinah glory!

> But [Yeshua] came and touched them and said, "Rise, and do not be afraid." When they lifted up their eyes, they saw no one but [Yeshua] only. As they came down the mountain, Jesus commanded them, "Tell the vision to no one until the Son of Man is risen from the dead."
>
> —MATTHEW 17:7–9

## MY TESTIMONY AND THE GLORY

As I shared in chapter 2, my mother unintentionally gave me the Hebrew name Meyer. Until recently I never knew the English translation had to do with being "a bearer of the light, or a bearer of the glory."

I have already shared the story with you concerning my background. But it bears the repeating of the essentials in relation to the Shekinah glory! As a little boy I was frightened of lightning and thunder. In order to comfort me, my sister told me about the existence of G-D. Though she was agnostic, she must have been compelled to share this to stop me from crying. She said, "He lives in a place called heaven, yet He is everywhere!" I became more afraid about this invisible entity called G-D who was ever present with me than I was concerning the lighting and thunder.

This triggered my childhood dream of seeing G-D in heaven. As I look back at this now, it causes me to realize that what I beheld was the Shekinah glory of the Most High G-D of Israel, the heavenly Father. G-D said to me, "Don't be afraid—I am your friend—I will never hurt you!" This dream was so profound, I tried to draw a picture of what I saw in my kindergarten class. (See the photo section.)

I also already shared that at eight years old, my mother took me to see Cecil B. DeMille's movie *The Ten Commandments*. When I saw the scenes where Moses stood in the midst of G-D's glory on Mount Sinai, it reminded me of that childhood dream. It was as if I was standing on Mount Sinai in the movie alongside Moses experiencing the presence of the Shekinah glory all over again. The presence of Him was overwhelming. That dream set me on a search to want to know the one true G-D of Israel.

---

## KEYS TO THE BLESSING

The Shekinah glory, according to the Word of G-D, is the actual presence of the one true G-D of Israel.

## STUDY QUESTIONS

What is the Shekinah glory?
[ ] Yeshua
[ ] The Ruach HaKodesh
[ ] The angel of the Lord
[ ] G-D the Father

What did G-D tell Moses was in the glory cloud?
[ ] A great anointing
[ ] Blessings and prosperity
[ ] A portal (doorway) to heaven
[ ] G-D's face

Whose voice did Peter, James, and John hear coming from within the glory cloud when they beheld Yeshua on the Mount of Transfiguration?

_____

_____

_____

## PRAYER

*Oh G-D of Israel, I ask that You allow me to encounter You in the Shekinah glory of Your presence. Please make Yourself real to me. I need You more than the air I must breathe to stay alive. I need You more than the food and water I need! I understand that one moment in Your glory can forever transform me. Please Lord, hear my prayer of desperation. I pray this in the name of Yeshua (Jesus).*

# Chapter 5

# THE ONLY MEDIATOR

In chapter 3 I shared the different levels of blessing and imparation we can receive through the Priestly Prayer of the Blessing. My prayer is that by the time you finish reading this book, you will understand how to fully experience the greatest benefits from this prayer. Let's review the seven levels of benefits once again.

1. One level of benefit comes from just reading the Word of G-D.

2. Another level comes by meditating on the Word.

3. Still a greater portion of blessing comes when we begin studying its deeper meaning and make a connection on how the verses relate to other passages in the Bible.

4. An even deeper level occurs when we study the Hebrew or Greek meaning of the words themselves. Often the English translators had to decide "what definition or shade" each word conveys in order to include the essence of what they have concurred is the correct meaning.

5. The next level is transformation as the Word of G-D affects our very thinking. In Scripture this is referred to as "the washing of water by the word" (Eph. 5:26).

6. An even deeper impact comes from an impartation from G-D Himself as His Holy Spirit writes the meaning upon our hearts.

7. But the greatest impartation comes when the person of the one true G-D manifests Himself—His very person—to us and dwells within us and upon us, and flows out from us to others! The result is a tangible change in our circumstances, and consequently we obtain supernatural breakthroughs!

I want to expound upon how we can receive the greatest level of impartation available as stated in level seven. I have already conveyed to you that the supernatural miracles that the children of Israel received for forty years in the wilderness came as a result of the Jewish high priest Aaron pronouncing the divine prayer over them every day. I explained why the Jewish high priest was the only one allowed to pronounce the Priestly Prayer of the Blessing over them, because there was only one mediator assigned to stand between the one true G-D of Israel and the people.

I further shared how the high priest was able to meet once a year in the holy of holies with G-D, the heavenly Father (who manifested Himself in the form of the Shekinah glory), and that by the proclaiming this prayer over the children of Israel, something very powerful would occur.

> [Through the proclamation of this prayer] they [the high priest of Israel and his successors] will put My name upon the children of Israel, and I will bless them.
>
> —NUMBERS 6:27

I revealed to you what it meant for the one true G-D of Israel to place His name upon them. Let me take this understanding deeper now. I must warn you. Some of you may not be ready for what I am about to share with you. I suggest you read what I am about to share, but if you are not yet ready to receive it, then please continue to read the rest of the book.

The other six levels of benefits I have listed above are something you will understand and receive without accepting level number seven. Perhaps at some later date you will be open to what I am about to share. But it is well worth your time to understand how to receive the full impartation of the full meaning of the only prayer contained in the Bible that G-D Himself wrote. It's important that you comprehend the full meaning of this prayer, which the English version in our Bibles doesn't fully communicate, but the *full impartation* is only available through what I am about to share with you!

## THE GREATEST LEVEL OF BLESSING

Since the fullness of the supernatural outpouring from the Priestly Prayer of the Blessing comes only when pronounced over us by the

Jewish high priest, there is a problem. Today there is no Jewish high priest that exists from the actual bloodline descendants of Aaron. With the advances of DNA testing, perhaps one day this might be possible. However, when it comes to having to trace generations so far back in time, the scientific precision required is lacking.

So how can we receive the full impartation of this blessing today—now—without a Jewish high priest proclaiming it over us every day? The good news is, though there isn't a Jewish high priest here on the earth today, there is a Jewish High Priest in heaven who desires to proclaim this prayer over us every day. His name is Yeshua (Jesus).

Yeshua as a Jewish High Priest doesn't have to perform all the things the high priest and the other priests (after the order of the Aaronic priesthood) had to do every morning according to Exodus 29. Yeshua doesn't have to make an offering for His own sins, nor wash Himself with holy water from the bronze laver, nor does He have to apply blood and oil upon Himself, because He is already holy and set apart to be the only intermediary between us and G-D the Father.

Again, in order for us to receive the full impartation of the Priestly Prayer of the Blessing, we must have a Jewish high priest to pronounce it over us. The problem remains is that there is no Jewish high priest on the earth today. Even if there was one appointed by the rabbinical authorities in the future, without the temple, the preparation needed for the high priest to minister cannot be accomplished without the Torah-compliant sacrificial system being instituted once again.

Furthermore, there is no guarantee that the one true G-D of Israel would once again fill the holy of holies with His presence in the form of the Shekinah glory as He has done in the past.

The Priestly Prayer of the Blessing resulted in such a powerful manifestation and supernatural power for the children of Israel as a result of the high priest of Israel proclaiming it over them every day. Aaron the high priest only had limited access into the holy of holies one day each year, during the feast of *Yom Kippur* (the Day of Atonement). How much more will we receive a greater portion and impartation of the person of G-D (the heavenly Father) Himself when Yeshua, our High Priest who dwells in the true "holy of holies," seated at the right hand of the Father twenty-four hours a day, seven days a week, pronounces this prayer over us every day!

So just as Aaron, as the high priest in Moses's day, was the *only mediator* between G-D and mankind in the holy of holies on earth, so too Yeshua (as our High Priest after the order of Melchizedek) is the *only mediator* between G-D the Father and mankind in the heavenly holy of holies.

> There is one [G-D] and one mediator between [G-D] and men, the Man [the Messiah Yeshua] Christ Jesus.
>
> —1 TIMOTHY 2:5

There is a holy temple in heaven with Yeshua, the Jewish High Priest who is of a higher authority than the high priest after the order of the Aaronic priesthood. Yeshua wants to pray this prayer over you today and every day!

King David prophesied of this heavenly High Priest:

> The LORD said to my lord, "Sit at My right hand."…The LORD has sworn and will not change, "You are a priest forever after the order of Melchizedek."
>
> —PSALM 110:1, 4

Yeshua HaMashiach (Jesus the Messiah) is seated at the right hand of the one true G-D of Israel (the heavenly Father) in the heavenly holy of holies. His throne is the mercy seat in heaven. Yeshua's own blood that He shed on the cursed tree was applied to this heavenly mercy seat so that we might receive forgiveness and become the children of G-D. (See Hebrews 4:14–16.)

At the last supper before His death and resurrection, Yeshua said the blessing over the bread and wine. This was the Hebrew blessing for the bread and the separate Hebrew blessing for the wine that all Jewish people are familiar with.

Many of us forget that in this prayer Yeshua is thanking G-D, the heavenly Father for His creating bread and the wine. Let us remember our heavenly Father as part of holy communion.

## THE BLESSING OVER THE BREAD

בָּרוּדְאַתָה יְיָ אֱלֹהֵינוּ

Blessed are You, O Lord our G-D,

מֶלֶךְ הָעוֹלָם

King of the Universe,

הַמוֹצִיאלֶחֶם מִן הָאָרֶץ

who brings forth bread from the earth.

## THE BLESSING OVER THE WINE

בָּרוּדְאַתָה יְיָ אֱלֹהֵינוּ

Blessed are You, O Lord our G-D,

מֶלֶךְ הָעוֹלָם

King of the Universe,

בּוֹרֵאפְּרִי הָעֵץ

who creates the fruit of the tree.

When Yeshua blessed the third cup of the Passover meal, which is known as the "cup of blessing" or the "cup of redemption," He said that this cup should be remembered as representing His blood—the blood that would be shed for the institution of a new covenant as promised in Jeremiah 31:31–33.

The mission of Yeshua before the cross was that of perfectly fulfilling (observing) every one of G-D's commandments in the Torah—without sinning once. He was the greatest old covenant prophet with the ability to heal, deliver, raise the dead, and perform miracles, signs, and wonders. His main mission was to be the suffering Messiah who would die for us as the perfect sacrifice, the unblemished Lamb of G-D, who was prophesied about in the *Tanakh* (Old Testament) scriptures to die and rise again! With His resurrection,

He became the firstfruits of many who would believe upon Him as their Messiah. (See 1 Corinthians 15:20–23.)

The mission of Yeshua would change after His resurrection from the dead. It was the beginning of His priesthood. As the resurrected one He walked with His disciples forty days after Passover. Standing on the Mount of Olives with His disciples before He ascended into heaven, Yeshua lifted both of His hands—the first time the Bible records Him lifting *both* hands—over them. Then it says that Yeshua proceeded to proclaim a blessing over them.

> Then He led them out as far as Bethany, and He lifted up His hands and blessed them. While He blessed them, He parted from them and was carried up into heaven. Then they worshipped Him, and returned to Jerusalem with great joy, and were continually in the temple, praising and blessing [G-D]. Amen.
>
> —LUKE 24:50–53

What was this blessing that Yeshua said over them? Yeshua had spoken the Hebrew blessings over the bread and wine during the Passover meal—His last supper. Here He was standing before His disciples *lifting up both hands.* There is only one prayer in Judaism where both hands are raised to proclaim a blessing. It is what the high priest did when he pronounced the Priestly Prayer of the Blessing over the children of Israel. The high priest of Israel would lift his hands in the form of the *El Shaddai* (meaning G-D Almighty).

Painting of Yeshua (Jesus) praying the Priestly Prayer of the Blessing over the disciples before He ascends to heaven (Luke 24:50–53). Painting courtesy of Deena A. Shuffler.

When I saw this truth, I was overcome with emotion as I understood what Yeshua was doing as His last act of ministry on planet Earth. Yeshua lifted both His hands in the same manner of Aaron the high priest and pronounced the Priestly Prayer of the Blessing over the disciples. He didn't do this as a high priest after the order of Aaron, but as the resurrected one, performing this as the High Priest after the order of Melchizedek—an everlasting priesthood.

There is no better explanation of the blessing that Yeshua pronounced over them that day on the Mount of Olives. This was the first priestly function of Yeshua. And while He proclaimed it over them, He ascended before their eyes into the clouds to take His position—seated at the right hand of G-D the Father. Yeshua's throne is the heavenly mercy seat (the throne of mercy) in the heavenly holy of holies.

Yeshua desires to proclaim the Priestly Prayer of the Blessing over you so you too can receive the fullness of impartation available.

Painting of Yeshua (Jesus) as our High Priest praying the
Priestly Prayer of the Blessing over us from the heavenly throne room.
Painting courtesy of Deena A. Shuffler.

## WOULD YOU LIKE YESHUA TO PRAY THIS PRAYER OVER YOU?

Before He can do that, you must first recognize Him as your Messiah (*Mashiach*), your Lord (*Adonai*), and your High Priest after the order of Melchizedek (Heb. 5:9–10). If you desire to do this, you can say the following prayers as an example, or simply pray (talk to G-D) in your own words that express what you feel in your heart.

*I come to You, G-D of Israel, and humble myself before You. I repent of my sins (my rebellion) against You and now desire to embrace what You call holy. I accept the invitation of Yeshua to sync my life with His. I accept Him as my Messiah, Lord, and High Priest by faith according to His invitation.*

Yeshua said, "Come to Me, all you who labor and are heavily burdened, and I will give you rest. Take My yoke upon you, and learn from Me, for I am meek and lowly in heart, and you will find rest for your souls. For My yoke is easy, and My burden is light" (Matt. 11:28–30).

*Yeshua (Jesus), I come to You, for I have been laboring, and I have been under a heavy burden! You promised that if I take Your yoke (figuratively a wooden crosspiece that is fastened over the necks of two animals) upon me (Your invitation to sync my life to Yours) that You will give me rest. Now I will walk alongside You and get to know You, for You are humble and meek. I will learn everything about You—what You taught, how You lived, and what the future holds for me. I will take counsel with Your written instructions (the Bible), and I look forward to when You return as King of kings! Your promise to me is eternal life and that walking with You will be easy and the burdens of this life will be light.*

If you prayed the above prayer or something similar from your heart, you have just become born again! Welcome to the family of G-D! Yeshua, your High Priest, will be the One who pronounces the Priestly Prayer of the Blessing over you every day.

Since you have now recognized Yeshua as your Messiah, Lord, and High Priest, He has given you something akin to the power of attorney to act in His name. When you have been given the power of attorney, you are acting on His behalf. It will be Him praying this Priestly Prayer of the Blessing through your mouth as you proclaim it over yourself and others. I will share several very important things about this as you continue to read the rest of this book.

+ You will discover the full meaning in Hebrew in what I call an "amplified Hebrew-to-English translation" of the prayer, which contains far greater promises and blessings than we see in the English translation contained in our Bibles.

+ You will understand how to pronounce this prayer over yourself and others in a manner that the one true G-D of Israel intended it to be proclaimed.

+ Finally, you will be able to have this prayer imparted by having it sung over you in ancient Hebrew. You will realize that the supernatural impartation of the name (the person of) the one true G-D of Israel will be placed upon you, and you will begin to experience the blessings and promises of the only prayer in the entire Bible that G-D Himself wrote.

I have included the URL where you can listen and watch a recording of the amplified Hebrew-to-English Priestly Prayer of the Blessing being spoken over you and then sung over you in the name of Yeshua, the High Priest (www.WarrenMarcus.com/prayer). It is an anointed version of the divine prayer sung over you in Hebrew by a world-renowned Messianic worship leader, Paul Wilbur.

## KEYS TO THE BLESSING

Yeshua, as the suffering Messiah knowing He would die on the cross for our sin, blessed the Passover *matzah* (bread) and the wine with the Hebrew prayers that all Jewish people recite. After the resurrection Yeshua, as our High Priest after the order of Melchizedek, lifted both hands in the form of the Hebrew letter *shin* (which stands for *El Shaddai*, Almighty G-D), and He pronounced over the disciples in Hebrew the Priestly Prayer of the Blessing.

## STUDY QUESTIONS

What does it mean that Yeshua is the only mediator between G-D and mankind?

What does it mean for you as a believer in Messiah Yeshua to have power of attorney under the authority of the one true G-D?

_____

_____

_____

## PRAYER

*Dear G-D of Israel, heavenly Father, I have recognized Yeshua (Jesus) as my Messiah, Lord (Adonai), and High Priest. I realize that it is He who will be praying the Priestly Prayer of the Blessing over me from His throne in the heavenly holy of holies. Through this divine prayer I am ready to experience You, my heavenly Father, in a more intimate, experiential, and supernatural way. I thank You for helping me grasp the fullness of what You have in store for me today and in my future. I pray this in the name of Yeshua (Jesus).*

## Chapter 6

# THE POWER OF THE
# HEBREW LANGUAGE

W<small>E'VE ALREADY INVESTIGATED</small> several of the questions that had troubled me concerning why my friend Rick Amato had been so affected by the Priestly Prayer of the Blessing. We know that it wasn't because Rick was so near the place of discovery. There wasn't a special portal to the heavens! Neither was there a special power concerning the amulet itself.

We have learned the importance of why only the Jewish high priest was allowed to proclaim the divine prayer daily over the children of Israel instead of Moses. We began to explore what it means that the one true G-D of Israel placed His name on the children of Israel.

I shared that though there is no Jewish high priest available on the earth today to pronounce this prayer over us, there is a Jewish High Priest available in heaven. Yeshua (Jesus) is our High Priest, and He desires to proclaim this prayer over you and me.

In my continuing search for why Rick had been so affected by the prayer, one question remained: *What about the fact that the Priestly Prayer of the Blessing was said over him in Hebrew and not English?*

As I reviewed Rick's words from the telephone call, I remembered that he said that the Priestly Prayer of the Blessing was proclaimed over him *in Hebrew* by the one who discovered the amulet, Gabriel Barkay. That's when I began to search the Hebrew text of this prayer for something that was missed when it was translated into English. As I studied the Hebrew, I quickly realized a far deeper, more powerful meaning than that which we read in our Bibles. Though the English translation of the prayer is beautiful, it doesn't impart the full anointing that my friend Rick experienced.

G-D led me to create an amplified Hebrew-to-English translation of the prayer, which I will be sharing with you as you read the rest of this book. As I began to pronounce the prayer over myself every day in this new amplified translation, I was personally impacted in a manner like never before. The prayer continues to bring a powerful experiential sense of G-D's presence, and it has opened a new, more intimate relationship with the one true G-D of Israel as my heavenly Father. It has allowed me to access the promises and blessings of G-D's divine prayer of unmerited grace!

After I experienced the profound effects of the prayer, I began to pronounce the amplified Hebrew-to-English translation of the prayer over others. All who experienced it were deeply impacted. It touched them far more than when I recited the prayer over them as it is expressed in our English Bibles.

One day I was introduced to a special recorded version of the Priestly Prayer of the Blessing sung in Hebrew by a world-renowned Messianic worship leader. As I listened to this recording, the impact was far greater than anything I have ever experienced before. I am convinced it is because of the fullness of meaning hidden in the Hebrew words. We are missing the fullness of meaning of the only prayer in the entire Bible that G-D Himself wrote. We are not receiving the fullness of impartation because the English translation we have in our Bibles is lacking the power and anointing.

I began playing this recording of the prayer being sung in Hebrew over others and discovered that the supernatural impartation Rick had experienced was now accessible to everyone who desired it. With the prayer pronounced over others in the Hebrew-to-English translation G-D had given me and sung over others in Hebrew, it would affect them in an even greater way than Rick first received it.

## A Remarkable Discovery

Swiss scientist Hans Jenny, born in 1904 in Basel, Switzerland, used a tonoscope to explore the effects of sound waves displaying patterns on sand and on other matter when played through piezoelectric amplifiers.

The remarkable thing he discovered was that the sound waves of the ancient Hebrew language reproduced and formed patterns in the sand close to the letters of the Hebrew being played through the tonoscope. Languages such as English, Greek, and French didn't have the same effect.[1]

In the Book of Genesis we are told that G-D spoke things into existence in the creation of the heavens and the earth, "And the earth was without form, and void; and darkness was upon the face of the deep. And the Spirit of [G-D] moved upon the face of the waters. And [G-D] said, Let there be light: and there was light" (Gen. 1:2–3, KJV).

The ancients believe that G-D (*Elohim*) spoke in the Hebrew language and its creative power supernaturally caused the heavens, the earth, and everything upon it to be formed. Not only does the Hebrew language contain multiple levels of meaning, but when it is spoken, proclaimed, or pronounced, the effects become tangible.

The Priestly Prayer of the Blessing in English is beautiful, but the *intended power* is lacking!

## ABSTRACT AND CONCRETE WORDS

In English and Greek there are many abstract words. In Hebrew there are very few abstract words. There is a depth to the words in Hebrew that does not translate into the abstract language of English or other languages.

The Hebrew words not only deal with our intellect, but also with our five senses. In English the following words in italics are abstract:

> The LORD *bless* you and *keep* you; the LORD make His *face* to *shine* upon you, and be *gracious* unto you; the LORD *lift* His *countenance* upon you, and give you *peace*.
>
> —NUMBERS 6:24–26

What does it mean for G-D to bless us or to keep us? How does He make His face to shine upon us? What does it mean that He will be gracious to us? How can He lift His countenance upon us? What does it mean by peace? These are abstract words, and we need to understand the Hebrew meaning in order to truly grasp what this prayer expresses.

Hebrew words are *not* abstract; they are concrete, meaning they relate to the five senses. They do not just create head knowledge; instead they affect the mind, soul, spirit, and even the members of our body.

When we receive Yeshua, we receive Him in our hearts and spirits, not through our heads. It's beyond an intellectual understanding of who He is. It's about knowing the person of Yeshua in a personal and intimate way.

It is tragic today that we receive Yeshua into our hearts and in our spirits, but then we spend the rest of our lives trying to understand things with our minds.

> But this shall be the covenant that I will make with the house of Israel after those days, says the LORD: I will put My law [Torah] within them and write it in their hearts; and I will be their [G-D], and they shall be My people.
>
> —JEREMIAH 31:33

Concerning the old covenant, the children of Israel didn't have the Ruach HaKodesh (Holy Spirit) within as their teacher, their guide, and one who empowered them to walk in obedience to G-D's commandments. Through the new covenant G-D helps us to understand His Torah (precepts, commandments, and revelation) and etches it onto our hearts. The abstract becomes experiential and concrete.

Every fiber of our being can be affected by the very person of the one true G-D of Israel—we don't have to walk alone. The first and greatest commandment shares that we are to love (have a relationship with) G-D that affects every part of our being.

> You shall love the Lord your [G-D] with all your heart, and with all your soul, and with all your mind, and with all your strength. This is the first commandment.
>
> —MARK 12:30

Hebrew thought is more concrete. This means in biblical Hebrew words are related to the five senses: sight, smell, sound, taste, and touch.

The goal is to receive these truths in our hearts, not just in our heads (Jer. 31:33).

Hebrew isn't void of abstracts; however, the abstracts are related to something that is concrete. An abstract is something that cannot be experienced through the five senses.

> The judgments of the LORD are...sweeter also than honey and the honeycomb.
>
> —PSALM 19:9–10

Oh, taste and see that the LORD is good...

—PSALM 34:8

These verses refer to the Word of G-D being like honey to our souls.

Many times the teachings we read in books or hear being preached from the pulpit are dealing with abstract concepts of the Word of G-D. The teachings titillate us and may move us as we hear or read them, but they aren't memorable. They're like riding on a roller coaster. It was thrilling while we were on it, but we can't remember what it truly was like because it didn't have substance.

As a TV and film producer of inspirational programs and movies, I can truthfully say that I have heard many teachers and preachers who were quite engaging as I listened to their teachings. Yet, after they finished, I tried to remember what was the essential truth they were sharing, but I couldn't recall it. I would ask others, and they would essentially communicate the same conclusion. We'd end up saying, "I guess I should buy their book or audio teaching to hear it again because as I was listening, it was so good." The truth is that it was more experiential, titillating the soul and stimulating the mind, but it truly wasn't transformational.

The apostle Paul, with the knowledge of his Jewish roots, talks about praying from the deepest part of your being!

> Likewise, the Spirit helps us in our weaknesses, for we do not know what to pray for as we ought, but the Spirit Himself intercedes for us with groanings too deep for words.
>
> —ROMANS 8:26

When the enemy of our souls attacks us, often we sense emotional upheaval that manifests as a physical attack deep down below in our bellies. Paul refers to the "bowels of mercies" in Colossians 3:12 as the place of deep-seated emotion. G-D can be experienced in the deepest level of our beings.

> Put on therefore, as the elect of [G-D], holy and beloved, bowels of mercies, kindness, humbleness of mind, meekness, long-suffering; forbearing one another, and forgiving one another, if any man have a quarrel against any: even as the Messiah forgave you, so also do ye.
>
> —COLOSSIANS 3:12–13, KJV

Mature believers use more than their minds!

> For everyone who partakes only of milk is unskilled in the word
> of righteousness, for he is a babe. But solid food belongs to those
> who are of full age, that is, those who by reason of use have their
> *senses* exercised to discern both good and evil.
>
> —HEBREWS 5:13–14, NKJV

As a mature believer you don't just have your mind trained to discern good and evil, but your senses have been exercised to discern the things of G-D. In other words, G-D can become so real to you that you can sense things as you drive in your car, enter a building, or hear someone talking. You may not have your Bible in front of you, but you can discern what is good and what is evil.

I remember attending a church service where many were deeply worshipping G-D. A woman came over to me and said, "Do you smell the roses?" At first I looked at her as if she were crazy. As I continued worshipping, suddenly I began to smell them too. I began questioning others around me, but they couldn't smell them. Others I have known have their senses so exercised that they can smell evil. You might be questioning whether such things are possible, but that's what Paul was referring to in the Scriptures.

The Greek mind-set deals with an intellectual pursuit of concepts and theology rather than how it affects the whole person—the mind, heart, soul, and strength.

Some people say you should not go by feelings at all, but only what the Word of G-D says. Yet the Holy Spirit can communicate to us through our emotions, which are beyond the intellect, but instead are tangibly experienced by us. We can sense when someone is sharing with us something that isn't right. We can feel the presence of G-D when we worship. We can actually experience joy or sadness that the Lord Himself is allowing us to experience!

Those who have been born again have received the "fruit of the Spirit" (Gal. 5:22–23). *Fruit* is the tangible evidence that hangs on a tree that demonstrates to everyone what kind of tree it is. You can be told that you are looking at an apple tree, but if there is no fruit displayed, then a person has every right to question whether this is truthful or not. Fruit is the outward evidence that can be seen, heard, felt, smelled, and tasted.

Someone can say they have joy, but if they don't, it will not be tangibly displayed for others to see. When you are going through a trial and you don't sense the peace of G-D, or you are struggling in your walk, by all means read the Word of G-D and cling to the promises G-D has for you.

Don't go by the negative feelings or by your emotions alone. If you are trying to make a decision that you feel good about, but it doesn't line up with the Word of G-D, then trust the Word above any feelings.

But my main point is that G-D wants us to experience His goodness. The "fruit of the Spirit" mentioned in Galatians 5:22–23 is "love, joy, peace, patience, gentleness, goodness, faith, meekness, and self-control." These are godly things that we can tangibly feel and experience. They are not just concepts. They are called "fruit" because they're the tangible evidence that others can see through our witness.

If someone says to you that they love you, but you don't feel that love or they are abusive to you, then you can be sure it isn't love. Love is something you can define with words, but you can also sense in a tangible way. If someone says they have the "joy of the Lord," but in truth they are continually critical, angry, and depressed, then you can be sure they don't have godly joy. Godly joy is something you can feel, even when the world around you is in turmoil.

The Hebrew language deals with the meaning of words and biblical concepts in the concrete, not just theoretical thinking. One of the main reasons Yeshua taught biblical concepts using parables was because these stories would help register and give meaning to these truths in a more practical way.

In the next chapter we will explore the first word we must understand in the prayer—the actual Hebrew name of the one true G-D of Israel. He has a name unlike any other name. There is power in His name. Those who are followers of the promised Jewish Messiah, Yeshua, understand that there is power in His name too. Yet Yeshua Himself talked a lot of the power in the name of His Father, the one true G-D of Israel.

## KEYS TO THE BLESSING

The Hebrew language is unlike any other. Most languages deal primarily in the abstract, but Hebrew conveys the concrete—the five senses—and deals with the mind, the heart, the soul, and every member of our being.

## STUDY QUESTIONS

What did scientist Hans Jenny discover about the ancient Hebrew language when he played it through the tonoscope?

_____

_____

_____

Are we created to experience and actually feel the evidence of the fruit of the Holy Spirit, including love, joy, and peace, or are these merely abstract concepts in the Word of G-D?

_____

_____

_____

# SECTION III:
# PRAYING IN THE NAME

## Chapter 7

# THE HEBREW WORD FOR NAME

THE NEXT SEVERAL chapters of this book deal with a very important subject: not just knowing *about* your heavenly Father, but instead getting to truly *know* Him and have access to Him in a supernatural, experiential, and intimate way.

How can we truly say we have intimacy with someone if we don't know what his or her name is? How can we declare we *know* G-D if we don't comprehend how much He loves us and how calling on His name will forever change every moment of every day of the rest of our lives? Let me assure you that other than understanding the full meaning of the Hebrew words of the Priestly Prayer of the Blessing itself, knowing the name and the character of the one true G-D as our heavenly Father will help you enter into a deeper, life-changing relationship with Him. After all, our heavenly Father is the one who authored this unparalleled supernatural prayer! To know our heavenly Father by His name will cause you to have faith to believe Him for the impossible!

In our English Bibles the word used for the name of G-D is LORD. It appears three times in the Priestly Prayer of the Blessing.

> The LORD bless you and keep you; the LORD make His face to shine upon you, and be gracious unto you; the LORD lift His countenance upon you, and give you peace.
> —NUMBERS 6:24–26

To more fully comprehend the power of the blessing, we must first understand the very name that is being placed upon us through the proclamation of G-D's divine prayer. How can we really truly obtain the full power and impartation of this prayer if we do not realize whose name is being placed upon us?

As I came to the realization that I didn't truly understand who the person is behind the very name that was being placed upon the children of Israel in this prayer of blessing, I reached out to my

friend Rick Amato. One of the things I knew about Rick is that he
had studied about and had been fascinated with the name of the one
true G-D for years.

He had written many pages of notes detailing his study about the
name, but he told me that years ago he had these handwritten notes
with him on an airplane and inadvertently, he had left them in the
pocket of the airline seat. He had already driven back toward his
home when suddenly he realized that he didn't have his study notes.
He drove thirty-five minutes back to the baggage claim. Rick was
obviously distressed, but the woman behind the desk didn't appear
to be sympathetic.

He asked, "Are you a believer in Jesus?" She indicated that she was.
Rick asked if she would join him in prayer that the notes might be
found. She did join him, and two other women hearing them praying
also joined in agreement with them. Then the woman entered into
her computer the information about the paperwork in case someone
cleaning the airplane might find it. Three days later, Rick got a call
from a man from Thailand who happened to sit in Rick's seat on the
next flight. He said he looked over the material and sensed something supernatural that compelled him to get the notes back to Rick.
That was twenty years ago.

Rick told me that after he had the Priestly Prayer of the Blessing
pronounced over him in Israel, he remembered those notes on the
name of the one true G-D. He searched for them, knowing that he
had moved several times. He had no idea where the important notes
could be.

Then one day I received a call from Rick, and he was shouting,
"Glory! Glory! Twenty years ago a man returned my study notes concerning the sacred name of the Most High G-D of Israel, and today,
twenty years later, I opened a box in my garage and there they were
in full view!"

Remarkably, twenty years from the day he had the notes returned
to him, Rick found them again in his garage. This happened in the
midst of my intense study concerning the Priestly Prayer of the
Blessing and my trying to understand the truth concerning G-D's
sacred name. I believe it is significant and indicates that understanding the name of G-D is the first step to receiving the full impartation of the divine prayer.

The first thing we need to comprehend is that there is only one true G-D, and He, like all of us, has a name. The first commandment of the Ten Commandments is:

> You shall have no other gods before Me.
>
> —Exodus 20:3

This clearly indicates that we should have *no other gods* before us except for the one true G-D of Israel. There's one G-D, and there are many false gods. These other gods cannot help us. They are either idols, which aren't living beings, or they are false gods—demons—who are trying to keep us from knowing the one true G-D. The Scriptures share the futility of trusting in false gods and idols:

> Their idols are silver and gold, the work of men's hands. They have mouths, but they cannot speak; eyes, but they cannot see; they have ears, but they cannot hear; noses, but they cannot smell; they have hands, but they cannot feel; feet, but they cannot walk; neither can they speak with their throat.
>
> —Psalm 115:4–7

We must be clear about who the one true G-D is. When we truly understand who He is and what it means to have His holy and sacred name placed upon us, it is life transforming! This knowledge alone has changed my life and opened up greater understanding of the Word of G-D. Scripture in the Tanakh (Old Testament) and in the New Testament have a new, powerful meaning and clarity. Furthermore, understanding G-D's sacred name and speaking it out loud when I pray has resulted in a greater intimacy and power in seeing my prayers answered.

## WHAT'S IN A NAME?

In most languages a name is a label, an identifier. My English name is Warren. It may have a deeper meaning, but we don't think of it as being anything more than an identifier.

This is not the case in Hebrew. Behind every Hebrew name there is a deeper meaning than the name itself. In Hebrew, names are made up of words. For example, the name *Ishmael* is made of two Hebrew words: *shama*, meaning "to hear," and *El*, meaning "G-D." Thus the name *Ishmael* means "G-D hears."

The biblical pattern of the naming of children generally falls into one of three categories:

+ A child's name is given by G-D.

+ A child's name reflects the parent's prayer for the child.

+ A child's name reflects the circumstances or character of the child.

Thus, a person spends his whole life under the identity of his name. Imagine naming your child Loser or Dummy. No one in their right mind would even think of doing such a thing. Why? Imagine the stigma of having such a name and what it would mean as other children made fun of your child. Imagine how your child would take on the identity of that word as you spoke it every time you called him or talked about him. In this sense the names that were given to people in the Bible often prophesied who they would become.

I have shared with you that my mother gave me a Hebrew name *Meyer*. The meaning of my Hebrew name is "bearer of the light" or "bearer of the glory." When this meaning was revealed to me, I was stunned. It's as if G-D's destiny for me to write this book was revealed in the Hebrew name my mother had given me.

The real name of G-D in the way that He identified Himself to Moses can be found in the Old Testament more than sixty-five hundred times. More than a label or identifier, it reveals something about His very nature and character. Therefore, it is very important for us to understand the meaning behind His name.

## THE TETRAGRAMMATON

Let's begin our journey to discover the full meaning behind of the Priestly Prayer of the Blessing by uncovering the meaning of the very first word. The actual word found on the amulet, written in ancient Paleo-Hebrew, is in the form of the *tetragrammaton*, the four Hebrew letters *Yod, Hey, Vov, Hey*, transliterated as YHWH.

# יהוה

*Yod Heh Vav Heh*
(Hebrew is read from right to left)

Centuries ago, Jewish rabbis began the tradition of not pronouncing the sacred and holy name of G-D out of reverence for His holiness, which led to the tetragrammaton replacing the sacred name. By using only consonants and not revealing the vowels of the name, its pronunciation has remained a mystery for many generations.

In ancient Israel only the high priest was able to pronounce the sacred and holy name. He alone would declare it over the people. Remember that there was great separation in the old covenant between the children of Israel and the one true G-D. Only the Aaronic priests could go into the tabernacle, and only the high priest could go once a year, on the Day of Atonement (Yom Kippur), into the holy of holies where G-D appeared in the form of the Shekinah glory.

As a child I attended Hebrew school as most young Jewish children do. One of the things they taught us was the holiness of the name of G-D. The name of the Lord is to be feared.

> For I am a great king, says the LORD of Hosts, and My name is to
> be feared among the nations.
> —MALACHI 1:14

If a Hebrew Bible or hymnal was dropped on the floor, we were taught to pick it up and kiss it in reverence to the sacred name of G-D. If someone dropped the Hebrew Torah scroll, that person and the entire congregation were supposed to fast for forty days in repentance. Again, it is because the sacred Hebrew name of the one true G-D is so holy.

We were also taught that because His Hebrew name is so holy, even when we write His name in English, we should only write the consonants and leave out the vowels. Therefore, instead of writing "GOD," we would write "G-D." This emanated out of the spelling of G-D's holy name as it is expressed in the tetragrammaton, which again contains only the consonants and not the vowels of G-D's sacred name.

The sacred name is so holy as expressed in the tetragrammaton itself that to this day Orthodox Jews will substitute the Hebrew word *Adonai* (which means "Lord") when they read it in the Holy Scriptures. Adonai is a beautiful expression of the one true G-D, but it isn't His sacred name as revealed to Moses. Yet even Adonai is too close to the sacred and holy name, according to some Orthodox Jews who won't say it in public. Instead, they will say in their conversations, "May *Hashem* bless you." They will refer to Him in public as Hashem, which means "the name." (*Hashem* is comprised of two words: *ha*, meaning "the," and *shem*, meaning "name.")

As a Jewish man who believes in Yeshua as my Messiah and Lord (Adonai), my relationship with G-D has changed. I am no longer simply a child of Israel—a child of the patriarchs Abraham, Isaac, and Jacob—but I am a spiritual son of G-D, my heavenly Father. We who believe in Yeshua have received access into the heavenly holy of holies to stand before the one true G-D, our heavenly Father. We can stand in the presence of the Almighty!

> Let us then come with confidence to the throne of grace, that we
> may obtain mercy and find grace to help in time of need.
> —HEBREWS 4:16

Through the new birth we have been adopted as spiritual sons and daughters of G-D. Because of Yeshua's sacrifice, we can come boldly before the throne of grace without fear of the name. In light of what Yeshua (Jesus) did for us, we don't have to be afraid to call upon His name and pronounce the sacred name.

## THE NAME AS THE VERY BREATH OF G-D

Although we have freedom under the new covenant, it is important to understand fully what the meaning of the Hebrew word *shem* implies to us. Remember that in Numbers 6:27 the one true G-D of Israel says He will place His name (*shem*) upon us. To understand what this means, we must first gain an understanding of the word *shem*.

As with various Hebrew words I'll be discussing in this book, the Hebrew word *shem* means so much more than the word *name* means in English. For instance, one shade of the meaning is the Hebrew word *ne-shema*, which means "breath." This is part of the full understanding of how significant it is to have the name of G-D placed upon us.

> Then the LORD [G-D] formed man from the dust of the ground
> and breathed into his nostrils the *breath of life*, and man [Adam]
> became a living being.
> —GENESIS 2:7

When we read "the LORD G-D" in our English Bibles, the actual Hebrew word used isn't *Lord* but the tetragrammaton, YHWH, the sacred name of G-D. It is the Father who breathed into Adam's nostrils; He was imparting a portion of His very person to Adam.

> Then [G-D] said, "Let Us make man in Our image, after Our likeness, and let them have dominion over the fish of the sea, and over the birds of the air, and over the livestock, and over all the earth, and over every creeping thing that creeps on the earth."
> —GENESIS 1:26

It was G-D the Father imparting the essence of who He was to His created son, Adam.

In Hebraic thought your *shem* (name) is your breath, and *your breath is your character*. It is your personality. It is what truly makes up who you are.

Even without knowing the biblical meaning of the Hebrew word for name, we often begin to associate certain traits of character to a person. You might see a person named Ralph and another person says to you about him, "Oh yes, Ralph. He is a liar and a cheat. Stay away from him." Even though we often don't realize it, when we know the actual person beyond just their name or title, we tend to associate their character with their name.

I thank G-D that when we come into the new covenant, Yeshua's death makes it possible for us to overcome the bad character our names once represented. Whether a person has been a drug dealer, an adulterer, a prostitute, or a murderer, G-D "so loved the world that He gave His only begotten Son" so that they might become new creations and their names begin to take on a new persona. (See John 3:16.)

> For you were formerly darkness, but now you are light in the Lord. Walk as children of light—for the fruit of the Spirit is in all goodness and righteousness and truth—proving what is pleasing to the Lord. And do not have fellowship with the unfruitful works of darkness; instead, expose them.
> —EPHESIANS 5:8–11

## TAKING THE NAME IN VAIN

The second commandment teaches us not to take the name of the Lord in vain.

You shall not take the name of the LORD your [G-D] in vain, for the
LORD will not hold guiltless anyone who takes His name in vain."

—EXODUS 20:7

Since the Hebrew word *shem* for the English word *name* actually means "character," let us replace the word *name* with the actual
meaning in the scripture found in Exodus.

You shall not take the [character] of the LORD your [G-D] in vain,
for the LORD will not hold guiltless anyone who takes His [char-
acter] in vain."

—EXODUS 20:7

Taking G-D's name in vain is not about adding a swear word
to G-D's name. It's so much deeper. It's recognizing that, through
Yeshua, G-D's name is upon us, and we must behave in a way that is
consistent with His character. We are to be examples of who the one
true G-D of Israel truly is.

You see, in English we look at the word *name* in the abstract.
When we read, "You shall not take the name of the LORD your G-D
in vain," we surmise that it is talking about not using some curse
word or profanity in conjunction with His name. Though it would
be a good idea not to do so, the Hebrew meaning refers to G-D's
nature, His character, and the person who He truly is. It is really
conveying that if we are the children of G-D, we should not misrepresent who He is. We don't want to do those things that defile or
discredit our heavenly Father and His holy character.

In the church today this is seldom being taught. Most don't realize
what this scripture and others like it are truly conveying. "You shall
not falsely misrepresent the only one true G-D of Israel and the
Messiah Yeshua (Jesus)."

In other words, taking G-D's name in vain is misrepresenting His
character. If we confess Messiah, but we lie, cheat, and steal, then we
are taking G-D's name (His *shem*, His character) in vain.

## THE CHARACTER OF THE ONE TRUE G-D

Many people in the church today are on opposite sides concerning
grace and holiness. The Scriptures declare:

But as He who has called you is holy, so be holy in all your con-
duct, because it is written, "Be holy, for I am holy."

—1 Peter 1:15–16

The truth is G-D the Father, Yeshua, and the Ruach HaKodesh
(Holy Spirit) are persons of the *Elohim* (the triune nature of G-D).
Just as we have things we love and things we dislike or even hate, so
too does G-D. In the Torah, G-D calls the things He loves "holy,"
and the things He hates "sin." He loves the things He calls "holy"
because if we do those things we will have victory, provision, good
health, prosperity, unity, peace, safety, perfect love, everlasting life,
and much more. The things He calls "sin" will bring strife, sickness,
failure, poverty, dissension, war, loneliness, despair, suicide, everlasting condemnation, and much more.

There are those in the world who get upset with what the one true
G-D of Israel considers to be "holy" because it doesn't include some
of the things they might embrace. The truth is the heavenly Father
knows best!

If we want to have a good and intimate relationship with another
person, the first thing we do is learn the things they love and the
things they hate. We then intentionally try to do those things that
bring us closer, and we avoid those things that would divide us.

The moral precepts of the Law (the Torah) are still intact. The
things G-D lists as being holy were not changed when the new covenant was ushered in because they reflect His character, and the character of the one true G-D never changes. The Bible says:

For I am the Lord, I do not change.

—Malachi 3:6

Jesus Christ [Yeshua the Messiah] is the same yesterday, and
today, and forever.

—Hebrews 13:8

G-D's character, His attributes or perfections, don't change.
He is always good, loving, just, righteous, holy, all-knowing, and
all-powerful.

## KEYS TO THE BLESSING

The name of G-D is more than just a label or title. It refers to His actual person, His holy character, and His power and authority.

## STUDY QUESTIONS

What does the Hebrew word *shem* mean?

_____

_____

_____

When G-D says He will place His name upon us, what implication does this have for us?

_____

_____

_____

# Chapter 8

# THE SACRED NAME

Our English word *god* is very broad; it can mean any deity, including false gods. However, the one true G-D of Israel identifies Himself with an actual name.

The actual sacred name ceased to be pronounced around the third century BC. Rabbinical Judaism teaches that pronouncing the sacred name is forbidden except by the *kohen gadol* (the high priest) in the holy temple on Yom Kippur. Modern Jewish people never pronounce the sacred name as contained in the tetragrammaton, YHWH. Instead they use *Adonai* (Lord) or *Hashem* (the name). The Jewish Masoretic text uses *Adonai* in the place of the tetragrammaton, YHWH.

The problem remains that many times in the Holy Scriptures the one true G-D of Israel declares that His sacred name shall be known.

> For from the rising of the sun to its setting, My name will be great among the nations, and in every place incense will be offered to My name, and a pure offering. For My name will be great among the nations, says the LORD of hosts.
>
> —MALACHI 1:11

When we talk about G-D to others, how do they know what G-D we are talking about? The English words *God* and *Lord* do not define who the one true G-D of Israel truly is. For instance, Buddhists refer to the Lord Krishna and Lord Vishnu. The Hindus worship some thirty-three million gods and goddesses.

The Old Testament refers to the sacred name of the one true G-D as represented in the tetragrammaton more than sixty-five hundred times. Therefore, I would submit to you that it is important to know what He revealed as being His actual name. For only then can we communicate whom the one true G-D really is.

## LORD Versus Lord

In our English Bibles the tetragrammaton, YHWH, is translated as LORD. Notice that it is indicated by the use of small capital letters—LORD—as opposed to other names for G-D that are translated using the lowercase letters—Lord—elsewhere in the Bible.

It is interesting to note that those in the religion of Islam hold in high esteem the name of Allah. They consider that expression to be the "sacred name." However, there are many historical resources that dispute this fact.

> That Islam was conceived in idolatry is shown by the fact that many rituals performed in the name of Allah were connected with the pagan worship that existed before Islam....Before Islam Allah was reported to be known as: the supreme of a pantheon of gods; the name of a god whom the Arabs worshipped; the chief god of the pantheon; Ali-ilah; the god; the supreme; the all-powerful; all-knowing; and totally unknowable; the predeterminer of everyone's life destiny; chief of the gods; the special deity of the Quraish; having three daughters: Al Uzzah (Venus), Manah (Destiny), and Alat; having the idol temple at Mecca under his name (House of Allah); the mate of Alat, the goddess of fate....Because of other Arabian history which points to heathen worship of the sun, moon, and the stars, as well as other gods, of which I believe Allah was in some way connected to. This then would prove to us that Allah is not the same as the true [G-D] of the Bible whom we worship, because [G-D] never changes.[1]

Islam itself points out that Allah was the name used long ago even before the Torah was given to Moses by the one true G-D of Israel. Yet we know that the one true G-D revealed His sacred name to Moses from the burning bush.

The name *Allah* is used today in Christian Arab language Bibles, but they will admit that the use of this name merely is like the English word *God* and not at all the sacred name of the one true G-D of Israel. Yet today Islam holds the name of Allah to be the sacred name to such a degree that anyone who defames that name will be held accountable and judged guilty with a death sentence for blasphemy.

Many believers today do not understand who the one true G-D is and what His actual name is in a way they can explain it to others. If we can truly understand who we are praying to and how glorious He truly is—who He is concerning His character and what He is able to do because of His attributes—we won't be afraid, struggling with so many issues. We will increase our faith and peace knowing that we have a "Big Daddy." Through Him, nothing is impossible!

It's important to know His name—because there is only one true G-D. This is made known in the Ten Commandments, which says:

> You shall have no other gods before Me. You shall not make for yourself any graven idol, or any likeness of anything that is in heaven above, or that is in the earth beneath, or that is in the water below the earth. You shall not bow down to them or serve them; for I, the LORD your [G-D], am a jealous [G-D], visiting the iniquity of the fathers on the children to the third and fourth generation of them who hate Me.
>
> —EXODUS 20:3–5

When we begin to understand who our heavenly Father truly is, then we begin to grasp the power and glory we can be part of while living on earth. If we are in Yeshua—we believe in Him and have been born again—then by default, when we pray to the Father, we are praying to the one true G-D of Israel. When we pray to the Father in the name of Yeshua, even without understanding who our heavenly Father truly is—holy, above all things, all powerful—by default we are praying to the one true G-D of Israel.

> For you have not received the spirit of slavery again to fear. But you have received the Spirit of adoption, *by whom we cry,* "Abba, Father."
>
> —ROMANS 8:15

*Abba* is the Hebrew term for "Daddy." It's OK to view yourself as a little child when you go before your heavenly Father.

> And because you are sons, [G-D] has sent forth into our hearts the Spirit of His Son, *crying,* "Abba, Father!"
>
> —GALATIANS 4:6

When we do not know how to pray, especially when we are going through the heaviest of trials, feeling low and unable to even lift up our Bible to read, we can go before our heavenly Father and allow the Ruach HaKodesh (Holy Spirit) to pray through us with words we don't understand.

> Likewise, the Spirit helps us in our weaknesses, for we do not know what to pray for as we ought, but the Spirit Himself intercedes for us with groanings too deep for words.
>
> —ROMANS 8:26

When it comes to fully understanding the significance of the Priestly Prayer of the Blessing, the Ruach HaKodesh helps us to understand the Hebrew meaning of the words so we fully appreciate and comprehend how powerful and profound the prayer truly is.

We are commanded in Holy Scriptures to proclaim His true name, the sacred name of the one true G-D of Israel. The name that is concealed in the tetragrammaton.

> For from the rising of the sun to its setting, *My name* will be great among the nations, and in every place incense will be offered to *My name*, and a pure offering. For *My name* will be great among the nations, says the LORD of hosts.
>
> —MALACHI 1:11

This scripture is clear that all nations are to understand the name of the one true G-D. Yeshua came to show forth exactly who the one true G-D is. Yeshua was a manifestation of the character of the Father for all to witness and comprehend!

> Thus says [YHWH], the Maker of the earth, [YHWH] who formed it to establish it; [YHWH] is His name: Call to Me, and I will answer you, and show you great and mighty things which you do not know.
>
> —JEREMIAH 33:2–3

So the hidden sacred name of the one true G-D is actually in the original Hebrew Scriptures. In the Scriptures G-D calls out to us, beseeching us to seek Him and petition Him in prayer.

How do you call out to someone without knowing his or her name? If my wife and I are separated in a crowded room and she wants to communicate to me, it is helpful that she can call out my name, "Warren, where are you?"

What about when we need prayer? If I don't know another person's name, I might say, "Hey brother, can I ask you to pray with me about something?" It's far better if I know that person's name. Why? Because when I don't know another person's actual name, my relationship remains at a distance.

The same principle applies to our relationship with G-D. If we say we have an intimate relationship with the one true G-D, yet we don't truly know His name, how intimate are we?

## Avoid Extremes

Before we go further, let me clarify that I am not taking the position of the Sacred Name Movement where people argue about the exact translation and how to pronounce the name of G-D. There are two extreme positions in the church today, and both are wrong!

One group believes if you are not saying the Hebrew name of G-D in the way they believe it should be pronounced, then you are on the way to hell. They will even argue about the correct spelling.

The second group says that the only way to say G-D's name is in English. They contend that we should use the English name of Jesus and not the Hebrew name of Yeshua.

One time I overheard a person saying, "I am sick and tired of hearing people saying 'Yahweh' or 'Yehovah!' I'm sick and tired of hearing people call G-D 'Adonai.' And I really despise when people pronounce the Messiah's name as 'Yeshua.' It's 'Jesus!'"

I responded, "Yes, His name is pronounced 'Jesus' in America, but it's pronounced 'Hey-sus' in Mexico."

It's ridiculous to get into that mentality. If someone lives in Israel and prays to the heavenly Father in Hebrew or to Jesus in Hebrew—praise the Lord—it is beautiful. When I am speaking in America, I refer to both the Hebrew and English names of the Messiah, I will often call Him both Yeshua and Jesus as I've done in this book.

If you are a believer, it's OK to address Him in English as God or Lord. I don't want to place condemnation upon you.

> The important thing isn't how to say His name. Even Lucifer (Satan) knows how to properly pronounce the name of the one true G-D, but he doesn't *know* Him, nor does he love the one true G-D.
>
> What is important is that we try to understand the difference between false gods and the one true G-D of Israel. My search took me into grasping the meaning behind His name in the Hebrew!

I must confess that since I began praying with the full knowledge of the sacred name of G-D, understanding who my heavenly Father truly is, His very person in relation to Yeshua (Jesus) and the Ruach HaKodesh (Holy Spirit), my life has been radically transformed like never before. I used to view the Most High G-D of Israel, my heavenly Father, sitting on His throne in heaven, distant and hard to approach directly. But as I continued my search, I have found that His desire is to make Himself known to me, always reaching out, pursuing me, desiring communion, wanting to impart His very person, His holy character, His power and authority upon me! By pursuing Him and accessing His divine embrace and His life-giving breath, by default I have found myself walking in the supernatural blessings and promises in a powerful way!

I can honestly say that I have a moment-by-moment sense of connectedness with the one true G-D of Israel like never before in my life. Things have become so clear. My understanding of the Holy Scriptures and doctrine is not confused. I am cognizant of the reality of supernatural power to help me fulfill my God-given destiny and purpose.

The apostle Peter quoted the Tanakh (Old Testament) concerning the promise of the Ruach HaKodesh (Holy Spirit) who would not just reside within every believer but also would come upon all believers when the new covenant would come into existence. When you read the original Hebrew, the sacred name of the one true G-D is made evident in the tetragrammaton.

> The sun will be turned to darkness, and the moon to blood, before the great and awe-inspiring day of [YHWH] comes. And it will be that everyone who calls on the name of [YHWH]

will be saved. For on Mount Zion and in Jerusalem there will be deliverance, as [YHWH] has said, and among the survivors whom [YHWH] calls.

—JOEL 2:31–32

The exact translation or pronunciation of His sacred name in Hebrew has been a mystery for generations. The exact vowels for the tetragrammaton have been lost. Today biblical scholars have come to some consensus. Understanding what they have found has helped me to draw closer to the one true G-D of Israel like never before!

## THE SACRED NAME OF THE MOST HIGH G-D OF ISRAEL REVEALED!

Theologians have come to two main possibilities:

+ YaHWeH

+ YeHoVaH (translated as Jehovah in some passages of the King James Version)

Many use the truncated form of the sacred name, YaH. YaHuWsHua is a more recent assertion by some in the Sacred Name Movement, but it is less known and not supported by the majority of Hebrew scholars or by manuscript evidence. The sacred name of the one true G-D of Israel was revealed to Moses:

> Moses said to [G-D], "I am going to the children of Israel and will say to them, 'The [G-D] of your fathers has sent me to you.' When they say to me, 'What is His name?' what shall I say to them?" And [G-D] said to Moses, "I AM WHO I AM," and He said, "You will say this to the children of Israel, 'I AM has sent me to you.'"
>
> —EXODUS 3:13–14

The phrase in Hebrew, *ehyeh asher ehyeh* (rendered as "I AM WHO I AM" in English) derives from the imperfect first person form of the verb *hayah*, which means "I will be," and therefore indicates a connection between the name hidden in the tetragrammaton YHWH. YHWH is the "source of all being" and has "being inherent in Himself." Everything else is a contingent being that "derives existence from Him."[2]

In this book I have chosen to refer to the one true G-D of Israel's sacred name as YHWH (which is YaHWeH or YeHoVaH), so as not to become a stumbling block to your receiving the fullness of this revelation from the proclamation of the Priestly Prayer of the Blessing.

## Catholic Catechism Defines G-D This Way

"[G-D] is the fullness of being, of every perfection and without origin (beginning) and without end. All creatures receive all that they are and have from Him; but He alone is His very being, and He is of Himself everything that He is."[3]

This is a different concept than in Eastern mysticism. Eastern Mysticism and the New Age religions talk about god(s) and all of creation and the universe itself as being one. They convey that "we are all god." But the Judaic/Christian understanding is that YHWH, the one true G-D, exists as the self-existent One. We are made in His image and likeness so that we have free will to enter into a relationship with Him or choose to ignore this life-changing relationship.

Also, we should understand who the one true G-D of Israel truly is. He is:

**Omnipotent**—This means G-D can do what He wants. It means He is not subject to physical limitations like man is. Being omnipotent, G-D has power over wind, water, gravity, physics, etc. G-D's power is infinite, or limitless.

**Omniscient**—This means "all-knowing." G-D is all all-knowing in the sense that He is aware of the past, present, and future. Nothing takes Him by surprise. His knowledge is total. He knows all that there is to know and all that can be known.

**Omnipresent**—This means "all present." This term means that G-D is capable of being everywhere at the same time. It means His divine presence encompasses the whole of the universe. There is no location that He does not inhabit. This should not be confused with pantheism, which suggests that G-D is "one with the universe" itself; instead, omnipresence indicates that G-D is distinct from the universe, but inhabits the entirety of it. He is everywhere at once.[4]

## TESTIMONIES FROM PRAYING IN THE NAME!

One well-known minister of the gospel shared with me his testimony of discovering the sacred name of YHWH. As he performed intense studies for many years to determine what the missing vowels are, he had talked with several Hebrew biblical scholars in Israel, including Nehemiah Gordon. He became convinced that the proper pronunciation is "YeHoVaH." This was hard for him accept at first because a lot of his teachings throughout the years referred to the sacred name as being YaHWeH.

He began beseeching G-D for the truth concerning this. He received a phone call that a close associate from his ministry was admitted to the hospital with a life-threatening condition. Her family believed that it was time for everyone to say their good-byes to her.

He went to the hospital and saw her family and friends gathered in the hospital room preparing for the inevitable. He prayed out loud to G-D, "If Your name is YeHoVaH then please show me—I will pray in Your name, and if this is truly Your sacred name, then when I use Your name when I pray, heal her in front of everybody!"

He then shared what he was about to do with those gathered in the room. Out loud he prayed, "YeHoVaH, heal our sister in Your holy name." To the amazement of all gathered there, she immediately opened her eyes and came out of a comatose state.

Today she is still alive and totally healed. This convinced him that he had discovered the sacred name of the one true G-D of Israel.

I want to point out to you that we who are in the new covenant are adopted spiritually as sons and daughters of the heavenly Father. It isn't as important to know exactly how to pronounce the true name of the heavenly Father—whether you use the more accepted YaHWeH or YeHoVaH—it is more important that we know Him and communicate with our heavenly Daddy. But I, and many others, have found that there is power in the Hebrew names that unlocks the supernatural power of the Most High G-D.

Another testimony comes from a woman that I know, who before she had a relationship with Yeshua as Messiah and Lord (Adonai), was involved as an exotic dancer in gentleman's clubs. When she became born again, she immediately stopped such activities. She began to study the Bible, go to church, and grow in her faith. Yet there was always a great conflict inside of her mind that remained for many years. The voices inside her raged, bringing conflict in her thought patterns. It affected her marriage and her role as a mother. She shared the difference it made of discovering and praying in the Hebrew names of G-D:

> This is what the Ruach HaKodesh (Holy Spirit) revealed to me. The perfect love I received when accepting Yeshua (Jesus) in my heart twenty-six years ago, the name of YHWH (YeHoVaH) is now my last name. When I was adopted spiritually by my heavenly Father, just as when a person is adopted they receive the father's family name, so too I know I have that new identity. I now belong to Him. That perfect love that He alone gave me, through various events that happened throughout my marriage, the enemy (Satan) used to attempt to destroy! Not only did he go after my marriage and family, through whispering lies within me, but the enemy also attempted to destroy the truth and my belief that YHWH's love is perfect. I had not yet understood these deep things to be able to have deliverance, confession, and repentance, so that His perfect love could be restored quickly. The enemy knew this perfect love is what utterly transformed me completely when I came to know Him at twenty-six years old. It was tiny little things hidden that Satan used to distort and twist, but grew over time. Once I began to understand the sacred name of the Father and prayed in that name, my breakthrough began to come. Glory to YeHoVaH for the revelation and restoration!

These are only two of the many testimonies I have received. There are many more that deal with supernatural physical, psychological, and emotional healing, prosperity, reunification of families, deliverance from demonic oppression and possession, divine provision, and so much more!

## KEYS TO THE BLESSING

The meaning of G-D's sacred name in Hebrew is "I Am Who I Am." He is the self-existent One!

## STUDY QUESTIONS

What are the two main ways scholars have decided to pronounce YHWH (the tetragrammaton)—G-D's sacred name?

_____

_____

_____

What is more important to know: the proper pronunciation of G-D's sacred name or the person of YHWH as your heavenly Father?

_____

_____

_____

# Chapter 9

# THE NAME OF YESHUA

MANY IN THE church today believe that the only way to say the Messiah's name is in English is "Jesus." But in other nations His name is pronounced differently. Jesus's name in Hebrew is accepted as *Yeshua*. In His full name and title *Yeshua HaMashiach*, we have a revelation of His attributes and character.

As a Jewish man I struggled with the English name, Jesus, when I became a believer. I knew He was the promised Jewish Messiah, and I accepted Him unreservedly by faith as my Messiah and Lord. But I did struggle with the English pronunciation of His name. The true horror stories of persecution of the Jewish people during pogroms, during the Crusades, and by Nazi Germany in the name of Jesus caused deep introspection and apprehension when we began singing songs of worship directly to Jesus.

As time went on, I got over my discomfort with His English name. Why? Because I intimately got to know the very person of my Messiah and Lord (Adonai). I didn't focus on the pronunciation of the name but on the person of Jesus.

Later I discovered Messianic Jewish congregations who used the Hebrew name of Jesus—that of Yeshua—to help unsaved Jewish people who might visit their Shabbat services to understand that Jesus is the promised Jewish Messiah. The premise is that by using the Hebrew name of Jesus, unsaved Jewish people who connected Christians and Jesus with the Holocaust wouldn't find belief in Messiah to be a stumbling block and instead might embrace Him as their Messiah and Lord by hearing His Hebrew name.

When I was first introduced to His Hebrew name, it was strange to me because I had by that time become familiar with the name of Jesus. I learned that the Jewish disciples called Jesus by the name of Yeshua, so as a Jew I began using His Hebrew name and found a deeper experience in my relationship with Him. Whether you like to refer to Him as Jesus or Yeshua, one truth I can attest to is that to know Yeshua is to love Him.

The formal name of the Messiah in Hebrew is actually *Yahu'Shuah*. At the time of Zerubbabel's rebuilding of the second temple, the name was shortened to *Y'Shuah*.

In English we call our Messiah and Lord "Jesus Christ." This is a label—an identifier—but it doesn't convey the attributes, character, or deeper meaning behind the name itself as contained in Hebrew. The word *Christ* isn't His name; it is His title.

The English translation of Jesus Christ came from the Greek, *Yesous Cristos*. *Christ* is the Greek word for messiah (*HaMashiach* in Hebrew) or "the anointed one."

*Yeshua* (*Yahu'Shuah*) means "YHWH saves." The sacred name of G-D is alluded to in Jesus's Hebrew name! You would never know that by His English name. Yeshua came to represent the Father. In the Hebrew name Yeshua the Messiah (the Christ), we have both His divinity as the only begotten Son of YHWH and the humanity of Him as Messiah (the anointed prophet). Yeshua is 100 percent G-D and 100 percent man. Thus, within the Hebrew name this reality is expressed, but the deeper meaning of His name is lost in the English translation.

> Jesus [Yeshua] said to him, "Have I been with you such a long time, and yet you have not known Me, Philip? He who has seen Me has seen the Father. So how can you say, 'Show us the Father'?"
> —JOHN 14:9

The full name of Yeshua HaMashiach (Jesus the Christ) means "the one true G-D saves as the anointed one—the prophet." He has provided us with direct access to the Father, and there is never any changing of this truth. Like YHWH (YeHoVaH or YaHWeH), Yeshua's being, nature, character, purposes, promises, and plans can be counted on, for He is faithful and true. He is the rock that we can build on, the One we can trust in this ever-changing world because He is one with the unchangeable G-D.

> Then Jesus said to them, "Truly, truly I say to you, the Son can do nothing of Himself, but what He sees the Father do. For whatever He does, likewise the Son does.
> —JOHN 5:19

> For I have not spoken on My own authority, but the Father who
> sent Me gave Me a command, what I should say and what I
> should speak.
>
> —JOHN 12:49

Yeshua was the living character of G-D the Father for us to see!
The words He said and everything He did were exactly what the
Father would have Him say and do.

Yeshua, the living Word, invites us to step into His yoke and
fellowship with Him. His identity—His character—begins to be
imparted onto us. As we get to know Him intimately. In essence we
are putting on the new creation; we are taking on His character.

> Come to Me, all you who labor and are heavily burdened, and I
> will give you rest. Take My yoke upon you, and learn from Me.
> For I am meek and lowly in heart, and you will find rest for your
> souls. For My yoke is easy, and My burden is light.
>
> —MATTHEW 11:28–30

Yeshua is saying, "Yoke yourself to Me." He is saying that He will
become the best friend you can ever have. He will not be angry with
you, abusive to you, or impatient with you. The very character of the
Father will begin to be imputed to you. It's a process of dying to the
old person we once were and the taking on of the new person who
G-D our Father already sees us as being, as He looks at us through
the nail-pierced hands of Yeshua. This is referred to as the process
of sanctification.

## WE'VE BEEN GIVEN A NEW NAME

In Yeshua we have been named with a new name. The name and
character of our old man (nature) has been exchanged for the "breath
of new life." The apostle Paul helps us understand the importance of
displaying the character of G-D for others. He said it this way:

> Brethren, be followers together of me, and mark them which walk
> so as ye have us for an ensample.
>
> —PHILIPPIANS 3:17, KJV

This was so hard for me to grasp as I read it. I felt that I couldn't
be like Paul and tell people to be followers of Yeshua together with

me. There were things in my life that I didn't want to be responsible for others to see and imitate. I thought Paul had to be such a holy person. I didn't understand the reality of the good news as I understand it today.

Today I can truly say to others, "Be a follower of the one true G-D as I am following Him." Why? Because the one true G-D of Israel is the one who does the transforming. Come and yoke yourself to Yeshua as I am doing, and watch what G-D will do in your life by the power of the Ruach HaKodesh.

I can be honest with others about how I used to be overcome with bad habits and sinful, hidden thoughts and actions that I hoped no one would discover. But through the process of sanctification, I have become an overcomer! There's hope in this journey through partnership with Him. I can be truthful and say, "Now I am struggling in this new area of my life, but He is helping me to be set free of this too. I am passing from one level of the glory onto the next." All praise goes to the Father!

As we walk with Yeshua, we have the covering of the name (*HaShem*) and the actual person of G-D on us and within us, by the power of the Ruach HaKodesh.

We aren't expected to be perfect, but we are on our way to perfection as we are yoked to Yeshua. We can call others to follow us as we follow Him! Likewise, we should seek out other believers who have overcome the issues we are facing or might still be grappling with.

While we are walking out our faith yoked to Yeshua, we can share our victories of overcoming with others, and be honest about the areas we are struggling to overcome.

Don't hang around people who are dealing with the sins or weaknesses you want to overcome. Instead choose to fellowship with those who are an example of the Messiah Himself, those who have overcome such obstacles by the power of the Ruach HaKodesh. Once G-D empowers you to overcome your weakness or area of sin, you will be an example to others who, like yourself, need the power of the Holy Spirit to overcome.

> Mark them which walk so as ye have us for an *ensample*.
>
> —Philippians 3:17, KJV

I quoted this verse in the King James Version because of the word *ensample*. (Other translations use the word *example*.) Even though their definitions are similar, I believe an *ensample* (or sample) is more than an example. An example is a representative of a pattern or group, whereas a sample is an actual specimen or piece of the group itself. It is like the difference between a picture of a material (an example) and an actual swatch of the material (a sample), something concrete that you can feel. If you want new wallpaper, it's one thing to look at a catalog for the right paper. But it is far better to obtain a small swatch of the actual wallpaper. You can get a better feel for what it looks like and even hold it up to the wall and get a better picture of how it will look on your wall.

There are people who are "ensamples" of Yeshua. They have come a long way in their walk, and hanging around them gives us a better idea of the reality of G-D Himself. The Holy Spirit makes the character of G-D real to us by revealing His character in the lives of others around us.

When we take the name of Yeshua upon us, we are called to be imitators of the Messiah. This doesn't come by our striving to become more like Him, but it comes through being in relationship with Him and having His character imparted to us by the power of the Ruach HaKodesh.

The time we spend in worship, prayer, and the Word (the Bible) causes us to obtain the power to become more like Yeshua. We cannot attain His likeness on our own, but only through the power of the Ruach HaKodesh within us. This truth is evident in the Tanakh (Old Testament) as Israel tried to attain righteousness without having the Holy Spirit within. They stumbled often, but G-D's grace was available to them for forgiveness.

How did the children of Israel obtain forgiveness? Through the sacrifices and offerings. This is the foundation of grace (unmerited favor) that was given in the old covenant, which is the same foundation of grace that we have in the new covenant.

In the church today many people try to be like Yeshua by following an old covenant form, that of traditions and outward rules, plus denominational doctrines of men. It's just not possible! It is only through an intimate relationship with Yeshua and by the power of the Holy Spirit within that you can begin to accomplish the impossible.

There are over 1,050 commandments in the New Testament. That's far more than the 613 commandments that the rabbis identified in the Tanakh (Old Testament). If you add on top of that the catechisms, the various denominational doctrines like those of Wesley, Calvin, and the numerous commentaries present in the various denominations of the church today, we can be easily overwhelmed.

Today in the church these man-made doctrines, added rules and regulations, have become more important to many than the Word of G-D itself! Theologians argue over these various doctrines of men. It makes the Pharisees of the old covenant look like "hyper grace" teachers by comparison. Most of the things in greatest contention between the various denominations aren't even in the Bible itself.

Before I accepted Yeshua as my Messiah and Lord, I would dialogue with a man named Richard Gallagher who had a table in the Port Authority Bus Terminal in New York City to compel people to sign his petition. I would pass his table every day on my way to catch a bus back to Linden, New Jersey. During the time I was attending the School of Visual Arts and my job as a film producer, cinematographer, and editor on Madison Avenue, I would daily interact with Richard, who was collecting signatures from people against abortion in order to solicit Congress to pass an amendment to reverse *Roe v. Wade* (the law that made abortion legal by the rule of the US Supreme Court.)

Richard was a Catholic believer, and I was an avowed liberal agnostic Jew at the time. I would often stop to debate religion with him. He was not polite to me. He argued incessantly with me. I would play the devil's advocate sometimes just to tweak him and provoke him to anger. Yet he knew his Bible and was able to stand his ground.

One day as I was talking with Richard, a Protestant Christian came up to the table and heard our conversation. This man had no idea that I wasn't a believer. He and Richard got into an argument about the mode of baptism. Richard said the Catholic Church performs infant baptism, while the other man said that baptism should only be performed when a person makes a decision to accept Jesus (Yeshua) as Lord. They got into a shouting match with each other. I couldn't take it anymore.

I spoke up in frustration, "The two of you are supposed to be Christians, but you can't agree with one another. How do you expect me, a Jew, to ever follow this man called Jesus when His church is in such a mess? You two are a perfect example of how screwed up religion is, and I don't want to have any part of it." I walked away from the two as they both stared at me in silence. Suddenly I felt a light touch on my shoulder. I turned around, and it was the man who had been arguing with Richard. He was teary-eyed as he began to speak.

"I'm a born-again Christian, and I want to apologize to you for what I did. If I had known you were searching, I would have never argued doctrine with that other fellow in front of you."

"That man's name is Richard, and he's really an OK guy," I said, defending him. But I was deeply touched by this man's sincerity.

"You see, you were totally right to say what you did to us," he continued. "But please don't judge my Lord and Savior Jesus by the way we acted. He is the only One who is perfect. There is nobody like Him. And without Jesus in my life, I would not be alive today, standing in front of you."

I never gave that man the satisfaction of knowing how his words impacted me. But the schism between the various denominations over doctrines of men is robbing the world of truly understanding that the one true G-D wants us to intimately know Him.

## THE POWER OF PRAYING IN YESHUA'S NAME

> I will do whatever you ask in My name, that the Father may be glorified in the Son.
>
> —JOHN 14:13

Many interpret this as if there is *magic* in the name of Yeshua. There is *power* in the name of Yeshua. But praying in His name means something far more!

What if we properly interpret the English word *name* from the Hebrew and Greek and substitute it for the word *name* in this verse?" It would read:

> I will do whatever you ask in My *character*, that the Father may be glorified in the Son.

If you ask G-D for something that is not in His character, you can be sure He will not do it. If you do receive what you asked for, but it is against that which G-D calls holy, then you didn't get it from G-D; you got it from the enemy.

How did Yeshua glorify the Father? By doing the things the

Father would have done on earth, by remaining consistent with the Father's character.

The Greek word for name (*onoma*) used in John 14:13 is consistent with the Hebrew word *shem*. *Onoma* means "the manifestation or revelation of someone's character so as to distinguish them from all others." Thus "praying in the name of Yeshua (Jesus)" means to pray as directed (authorized) by Him, bringing revelation that flows out of His being when you are in His presence. Let me repeat that with strong emphasis on one particular part of the definition: Praying in the name of Yeshua means to pray as directed by Him, bringing revelation that flows *out of His being when you are in His presence!*

Through being yoked to Him, you will receive communication from the Ruach HaKodesh to help you know what to do as you face various situations! When you pray, it's as if Yeshua Himself is praying through you.

"Praying in the name of Yeshua," therefore, is not a religious formula just to end prayers, or a magic word to get what we want! Praying in His name is praying in His actual person, with His holy character and in His power and authority. If G-D answers your prayer, then He is the One who receives all the glory, not you!

In Hebraic thinking, a name isn't a label or a tool merely used to distinguish one person from another. A person's name is viewed as equivalent to the person himself. A person's name signifies their person, worth, character, reputation, authority, will, and ownership. Everything they have and everything they are is reflected in their name.

Scripture records an account of some men who thought the name of Yeshua (Jesus) was a mystical formula or even magic. They thought they could use the name of Yeshua apart from pursuing an intimate relationship with Him.

> Then some of the itinerant Jewish exorcists invoked the name of the Lord Jesus over those had evil spirits, saying, "We command you to come out in the name of Jesus whom Paul preaches."
> —Acts 19:13

You see, they didn't know Yeshua. They were trying to take authority over evil spirits by saying the name of Yeshua—the person Paul preached about.

There were seven sons of a Jewish high priest named Sceva doing this. The evil spirit answered, "I know Jesus, and I know Paul, but who are you?"

—ACTS 19:14–15

The evil spirits recognized that these men had no authority because they were trying to use the name of Yeshua as a magic formula. But when we take authority in the name of Yeshua, what is actually happening is we are coming in Yeshua's actual person, with His holy character and with His power and authority. We are the vessels being used by Yeshua Himself to flow through and cast the demons out.

Then the man in whom the evil spirit was jumped on them, overpowered them, and prevailed against them, so that they fled from that house naked and wounded.

—ACTS 19:16

The evil spirit, knowing that these men had no authority, came out of the one possessed and leaped upon them, tearing their clothes off and wounding them. What a great scene in a movie this would make. I can see these men running out with clothes ripped, bruised from the beating they took, and shouting, "Let's get out of here!"

Although they attempted to cast out an evil spirit in the right name, because they were not believers who knew Him as their Messiah and Lord and did not represent His person, they were in effect attempting to cast out the evil spirits in their own authority and their own works, and they were not successful.

The evil spirit recognized this and would not submit. There is no magical power in just saying, "in Jesus's name," or "in the name of Yeshua." But when we truly understand that the power of G-D comes when we are agents for His person to flow through, then we will see miracles, healings, and deliverance begin to flow as a normal part of our spiritual walk.

I want to be careful not to let the enemy use what I am saying to discourage you from praying for others for their healing. If you have prayed in Yeshua's (Jesus's) name over people before (without realizing the fullness of what this means), don't allow the enemy to place condemnation upon you. Many first-time believers pray for people in the streets and the one true G-D of Israel is gracious because His heart is to see people saved, healed, and set free. The truth is G-D will use a donkey if He wants to deliver a message to someone as He did with Balaam! (See Numbers 22:21–39.)

We read how the apostle Peter took no credit when G-D moved through him and John to heal the sick.

> Now Peter and John went up together to the [holy] temple at the ninth hour, the hour of prayer. A man lame from birth was being carried, whom people placed daily at the gate of the temple called Beautiful to ask alms from those who entered the temple. Seeing Peter and John about to go into the temple, he asked for alms. Peter, gazing at him with John, said, "Look at us." So he paid attention to them, expecting to receive something from them. Then Peter said, "I have no silver and gold, but I give you what I have. In the name of Jesus Christ [Yeshua the Messiah] of Nazareth, rise up and walk." He took him by the right hand and raised him up. Immediately his feet and ankles were strengthened. Jumping up, he stood and walked and entered the temple with them, walking and jumping and praising [G-D]. All the people saw him walking and praising [G-D]. They knew that it was he who sat for alms at the Beautiful Gate of the temple. And they were filled with wonder and amazement at what happened to him.
>
> —ACTS 3:1–10

Peter prayed for the man in the name of Yeshua, and the man was healed. The man followed Peter and John into the holy temple in Jerusalem. The people gathered there were amazed because they recognized him as the man who sat crippled for years in front of the gate called Beautiful. They wanted an explanation as to what happened.

Peter could have said, "I am the mighty man of G-D who prayed in the name of Yeshua and he was healed. Everyone else here needs me to pray for you." But instead Peter said:

> Men of Israel, why do you marvel at this man? Or why do you stare at us, as if by our own power or piety we had made him walk? The [G-D] of Abraham and Isaac and Jacob, the [G-D] of our fathers, has glorified His Son [Yeshua], whom you handed over and denied in the presence of Pilate, when he had decided to release Him. You denied the Holy and Righteous One and asked for a murderer to be granted to you, and you killed the Creator of Life, whom [G-D] has raised from the dead, of which we are witnesses. And His [Yeshua's] name, by faith in His name, has made

this man strong, whom you see and know. And faith which comes through Him has given him perfect health in your presence.

—Acts 3:12–16 Peter took no credit at all for the healing that took place; he gave G-D all the glory. That's because He prayed in the *shem* (name) of Yeshua, not in the "magic" name of Yeshua, but as Yeshua's representative, allowing the person, authority, and power of Yeshua to heal this man.

The point I want to leave you with is, if we could truly grasp this biblical truth as believers in Messiah, then people in wheelchairs would begin praying for others in wheelchairs in the name of Yeshua. The lame would walk! Blind people would pray for others who are blind, and the blind would see! What if those of us who are under the new covenant began to understand that it isn't about us? We are just the vessels allowing the person of G-D Himself to flow through us. Imagine a man who is deaf praying for a woman who cannot hear and seeing her healed. It will demonstrate that it is G-D alone who did the healing, and He will receive all the glory and honor.

Yeshua by example said:

> For I have not spoken on My own authority, but the Father who sent Me gave Me a command, what I should say and what I should speak.
>
> —JOHN 12:49

In other words, when we start understanding that we are only "the vessels" for G-D Himself to flow through, then no matter who we are—man, woman, young, old, healthy, or handicapped—G-D will use us as His representatives on earth to demonstrate His glory and power.

The reason many believers aren't walking in the supernatural power of G-D is because many don't feel worthy to be used of Him in this way. The truth is none of us is worthy enough. But G-D wants to use you if you are willing to be the one who will pray in His person, with His holy character, and with His power and authority, and will make sure that He gets all the glory and honor!

Our English Bibles use *Lord* (from the Hebrew word *Adonai*), but now you know that the real word used in the Priestly Prayer of the Blessing is His sacred name.

[YHWH, YeHoVaH, YaHWeH, your heavenly Father] bless you and keep you; [YHWH, YeHoVaH, YaHWeH, your heavenly Father] make His face to shine upon you, and be gracious unto you; [YHWH, YeHoVaH, YaHWeH, your heavenly Father] lift His countenance upon you, and give you peace.

—NUMBERS 6:24–26

Now that you have an understanding of the powerful meaning of the name of G-D and the name of Yeshua, we are ready to move on to the next section of this book where we will break down the Priestly Prayer of the Blessing and reveal its deeper, hidden meaning as conveyed in the original Hebrew.

## KEYS TO THE BLESSING

In Yeshua we have been named with a new name. The name and character of our old man (*nature*) has been exchanged for the "Breath of New Life."

## STUDY QUESTIONS

What is Jesus's Hebrew name? What is the meaning of His Hebrew name?

_____

_____

_____

What does it mean for us to pray in Yeshua's name?

_____

_____

_____

# SECTION IV:
# BREAKING DOWN THE HEBREW MEANING OF THE PRAYER

# Chapter 10

# THE HEBREW WORD FOR BLESS

## בָּרוּךְ

*Barakh*, literally, "to kneel down"
(Hebrew is read from right to left)

T HE NEXT WORD in the Priestly Prayer of the Blessing is *bless*.

The LORD bless you.

—NUMBERS 6:24

Understanding the meaning of the English word *bless*, which is *barakh* in Hebrew, is so important because without this you will never receive the full impartation and complete implication of what this divine prayer can usher into your life.

We must overcome what could be a stumbling block in truly receiving the fullness of the promises and unparalleled impartation being offered to us! Receiving what YHWH (YeHoVaH, YaHWeH, the heavenly Father) has for us in the rest of this prayer is contingent on comprehending and accepting the meaning of this first portion alone.

Before writing this book, I developed a powerful two-part audio CD teaching and other ancillary material concerning the Priestly Prayer of the Blessing, including my own amplified Hebrew-to-English translation of the prayer. I asked a good friend of mine, a man of G-D whom I deeply respect, to read the amplified Hebrew-to-English translation of the prayer that I created.

When he read this first portion concerning the Hebrew meaning of the word *bless*, he said, "This is *not* possible!" It appeared to upset him, and he said, "This could offend others!" I began to explain the deeper truths I found biblically from my teaching to support what I was sharing, but he didn't want to hear it. He was insistent that this could become a stumbling block to people and they wouldn't get the rest of the benefits because of the interpretation I am presenting.

I knew in my heart he was wrong. I had already shared this teaching in congregations of various denominations and the presence of YHWH (the heavenly Father) always manifested so powerfully that the people would be deeply affected and dramatically transformed.

Yet because I deeply respected this man of G-D so much, his criticism troubled me and caused me to seek G-D in prayer. I was concerned over what he had said to me. For several weeks I continued to be deeply unsettled by his reaction. Yet it was this catalyst I needed to begin to realize the importance of truly understanding this first portion above all. G-D impressed upon me, "If one doesn't understand this first part, they will never receive the rest."

The English word *bless* is an abstract concept. Think about it, what does it mean to bless? Is it merely saying to another, "G-D bless you"? What does it mean when we say to the Lord G-D Almighty, "I bless You, my G-D"?

In Hebrew the word for bless is *barakh*. One of the ways we can better understand the meaning of this abstract word is by looking into how the word is used in other passages of Holy Scripture.

> He made his camels kneel down [*barakh*] outside the city by a well of water in the evening when the women came out to draw water.
> —GENESIS 24:11

The camel kneels down so that the person may receive the gifts that the camel is carrying on its back. Figuratively, kneeling down to help someone pick up something they have dropped is also "blessing" them.

This first portion of the Priestly Prayer of the Blessing communicates that the one true G-D of Israel is kneeling down in front of you to make Himself available to you in a way like you never thought possible. You will experience the greatest intimacy possible with YHWH (your heavenly Father) and receive all the gifts He wants to impart to you.

## SEE IT IN YOUR MIND'S EYE

Imagine YHWH kneeling before you as a good Father who would do anything for you, His child, desiring to demonstrate His availability to you. If you were a little child seeing your daddy kneeling in front of you, with his arms extended toward you, you would receive this as a clear invitation, beckoning you to respond.

This first portion of the Priestly Prayer of the Blessing involves G-D our Father making Himself available to each of us. It demands a response: Do we ignore Him? Do we just stand and look at Him kneeling before us? No! We are moved to respond in our hearts and humble ourselves and fall to our knees so we can receive His invitation! A child seeing his good father or mother kneeling in front of him would know that what comes next is their loving embrace.

The one true G-D of Israel wants to come down from His heavenly throne to be with you. This is actually what occurs when the Priestly Prayer of the Blessing is pronounced over you in the name of the Jewish High Priest Yeshua (Jesus).

The concrete or extended meaning of the Hebrew word *barakh* is "to do" or "to give something of value to another." G-D blesses you by making Himself available. He wants to provide for your needs, and you in turn bless G-D by giving Him yourself in submission as He kneels in front of you with His outstretched arms of love.

Many of us have need of healing, deliverance, salvation, or a financial or some other breakthrough! We often turn to G-D in our times of trouble and ask Him to answer our prayers. We move from one need to the next. But Yeshua talked about why we shouldn't be anxious for our daily needs:

> Therefore, I say to you, take no thought about your life, what you will eat, or what you will drink, nor about your body, what you will put on. Is not life more than food and the body than clothing? Look at the birds of the air, for they do not sow, nor do they reap, nor gather into barns. Yet your heavenly Father feeds them. Are you not much better than they? Who among you by taking thought can add a cubit to his stature? Why take thought about clothing? Consider the lilies of the field, how they grow: They neither work, nor do they spin. Yet I say to you that even Solomon in all his glory was not dressed like one of these. Therefore, if [G-D] so clothes the grass of the field, which today is here and tomorrow is thrown into the oven, will He not much more clothe you, O you of little faith? Therefore, take no thought, saying, "What shall we eat?" or "What shall we drink?" or "What shall we wear?" (For

the Gentiles seek after all these things.) For your heavenly Father knows that you have need of all these things.

—MATTHEW 6:25–32

The key statement made here is that YHWH your heavenly Father knows what you need before you even ask for it. What must you do to receive such favor of the Father?

But seek first the kingdom of [G-D] and His righteousness, and all these things shall be given to you.

—MATTHEW 6:33

We are not called to seek the kingdom as an end in itself. We are to seek the kingdom to be with our heavenly Father, who wants to supply our needs "according to His riches in glory" (Phil. 4:19). When we are with our heavenly Father, we receive everything we need. In Matthew 6:8 Yeshua said: "For your Father knows the things you have need of before you ask Him" (NKJV).

According to Yeshua the main thing we must do to gain favor from the Father is to "seek first the kingdom of G-D." Many books and teachings have been created about the kingdom of G-D, but I believe there is a misunderstanding of what Yeshua was referring to. When Yeshua said, "Seek first the kingdom of G-D and His righteousness, and all these things shall be given to you," He was conveying that we are to seek the kingdom of G-D, not as an end in itself, but because *the King* is there. He was referring to obtaining an intimate relationship with the one true G-D of Israel. When we are in the presence of our heavenly Father, we receive everything we need by default. We don't have to even ask because He, as a good Father, is with us and already discerns what we are lacking.

So many of us live from one need to another. We seek G-D's hand of provision instead of seeking His face. In 2 Chronicles 7:14 YHWH gives us a formula for truly obtaining healing and even revival to invade our land.

If My people, who are called by My name, will humble themselves and pray, and *seek My face* and turn from their wicked ways, then I will hear from heaven, and will forgive their sin and will heal their land.

Imagine what G-D is saying here! People first need to humble themselves. To humble oneself in the Hebrew sense is to come to the end of yourself and confess that you don't have all the answers, the power, or the means to survive without G-D in your life. The best way to describe it is receiving an epiphany or having an "aha moment" of revelation. King David humbled himself often before almighty G-D in his psalms.

> Be gracious to me, O LORD, for I *am* weak; O LORD, heal me, for my bones are terrified. My soul is greatly troubled, but You, O LORD, how long?
>
> —PSALM 6:2–3

> I am weary with my groaning; all night I flood my bed with weeping; I drench my couch with my tears. My eye wastes away from grief; it grows weak because of all those hostile to me.
>
> —PSALM 6:6–7

The injunction laid out by G-D in 2 Chronicles 7:14, after we humble ourselves, is to pray—to start communicating with our heavenly Father and talking with Him. But it doesn't end there. Most of us have come to the Lord at one time or another and prayed to Him. But it is the next part of that scripture that is truly different. The Father tells His people to seek His face. This is a call to deep intimacy.

If the Father is asking us to seek His face, doesn't this mean that we can have access to Him in the most intimate way? YHWH would not be so cruel to tease us, saying, "Seek My face," but then continue to hide Himself from us. G-D is *not* a liar!

Our heavenly Father is saying, "I want you to approach Me, to come into My presence. I want you to allow Me to be with you, to share My love with you. You have been distant—caught up in your busy life, yet here I am right in front of you—I want you to know how much I love you. I am waiting for you to tell Me, 'I love you, Daddy (Abba)!'"

I remind you about my childhood dream when I was transported into heaven and I beheld G-D the Father in the Shekinah glory. Not only was it the most beautiful thing I have ever beheld, as colorful beams of light pushed out toward me from the source of the beautiful golden light in the distance, but also I wasn't afraid. Instead I felt great peace and fulfillment. Then I heard G-D's voice inside of me and also outside of me as He said, "Don't be afraid. I am your friend. I will never hurt you!"

Satan absolutely hates the heavenly Father. Why? Because Satan was thrown out of heaven by the Father for rebelling against Him! Satan's main objective is to keep us away from intimacy with the Father. The devil has already been defeated by Yeshua at the cross. By recognizing Yeshua as our Messiah and Lord (Adonai), we can gain intimacy with Him and sense His presence as we commune with Him. Satan cannot stop the Ruach HaKodesh (Holy Spirit) from the work He is performing in our lives, once we have been born again. But if Satan could somehow discredit the heavenly Father and keep us from accessing Him, then he has a chance of thwarting our God-given destiny and purpose.

As I contemplated the reality of this first portion of the Priestly Prayer of the Blessing where the Hebrew conveys that the one true G-D wants to "kneel before me, making Himself available to me," I beheld this following vision.

## THE PARABLE OF THE HOMELESS MAN AND THE LIMO DRIVER

While worshipping YHWH, I had a vision. I believe this is a God-inspired parable. I envisioned a homeless man in his early forties walking on the busy streets of New York City on a hot summer's day. His face was unshaven and dirty. His clothes were disheveled and torn. He had his hand out begging for money as many passed him by, ignoring him. Some looked upon him with disdain.

The man cried out, "Oh G-D, help me. I am so hungry. I just need enough money to buy some food. Please, Lord, help me." Soon after praying this, a young businessman's eyes caught a glimpse of the homeless man as he walked toward him. The Ruach HaKodesh moved upon the businessman's heart with deep compassion.

He reached into his pocket for cash. All he had was a ten-dollar bill. He stopped in front of the homeless man and gave him the money. The homeless man gazed back into the eyes of the businessman as the businessman said, "This is from G-D for you."

The homeless man looked down at the ten-dollar bill that he now clutched in his hand and responded, "G-D bless you."

Then the setting changed, and I saw the homeless man sitting in the doorway of an out-of-business store, relishing every bite of the hamburger and french fries he bought with the ten dollars. He looked up to G-D and thanked Him for this answer to prayer. The next day he was back on the sidewalk begging for money to buy his next meal.

I sensed the Lord showing me that this homeless man represented many Jewish and Gentile believers in Messiah Yeshua today! We often live from one need to the next—beseeching G-D for an answer to our prayers as we face the circumstances in our lives. We seek G-D's hands but not His face. For when we seek true intimacy with our heavenly Father, He already knows *all* the needs we have and by default of being in His presence, we receive His forgiveness, favor, healing, and provision!

The homeless man was now begging for money to buy his next meal, but to no avail. He was surrounded by masses of pedestrians walking quickly past him, making their way to bus terminals and train stations as they traveled home after a hard day's work. The poor man felt it was as if he had become invisible. Tears came to his eyes as he realized this was his reality—a life of misfortune and circumstances beyond his control.

He turned again to G-D, praying, "Oh G-D, I can't do this anymore. I need You—I give up trying to do this on my own. I need You more than the food I need to eat. I need You more than the water I need to drink. I need You more than this stagnant city air I am breathing. Take me home. Life is just too hard! I can't do this anymore." Like King David in the psalms, this man had come to the end of himself.

Minutes after praying, while standing at the curb waiting for the traffic light to change, a limousine pulled up in front of him. The limo driver powered down his window and called out to him, "Sir!" The homeless man looked around thinking the driver couldn't be talking to him. "Yes, I'm talking to you." The driver got out of the vehicle and opened the back door, inviting the homeless to get in, "Come with me—I will take you to get some food."

The homeless man tentatively got into the limo. As the limo took off, the driver said, "There's a fridge back there with drinks. Take what you'd like." The homeless man wondered if he was dreaming as he took a bottle of cold water out of the fridge. As the limo drove through the city, the homeless man looked up to heaven and silently thanked the Lord. In the safety of the luxurious limo he soon drifted off to sleep. When he awoke, he found that the limo was driving on a scenic road in the mountains. The limo turned and entered a tree-lined driveway, which led to a high-walled property. A gilded gate opened automatically, allowing the limo access. The homeless man asked himself, "Am I dreaming? Am I dead and being transported to heaven?" The estate was beautifully landscaped with flower gardens, trimmed hedges, exotic trees, and large stretches of green grass.

The limo stopped at the entrance of the large exquisite mansion. The limo driver opened the back door, ushering him out of the vehicle, "Sir, please come with me. Dinner is almost ready." The homeless man followed the driver to the front door of the mansion and entered. He was suddenly surrounded by opulence, quite a different environment from the dirt-ridden New York City streets and back alleys that had been his home for the past several years. The sweet smell of fragrances filled the atmosphere, much better than the stench of the city streets and subways during the hot stifling summer days.

The limo driver beckoned him to follow him. As they entered the lavish dining room, he told the homeless man to take his place at the long banqueting table. The limo driver assured him, "The Master will be here shortly."

The Master entered the room. The homeless man beheld the awesome presence of the Master who exhibited a warm smile and piercing eyes that sparkled with warmth and acceptance. The homeless man rose to his feet as the Master approached him with his arms extended. The Master embraced the homeless man and held him close as the homeless man broke down weeping. The Master said softly, "You are home now!" He encouraged the man to be seated. The homeless man wondered if he had expired and now was in heaven.

The Master smiled, reading his mind, "No, you are not dead—this isn't a dream—this isn't your final resting place." As the seven-course meal was served by an array of hospitable angels, the Master began to impart scriptures from the Word of G-D to build the homeless man's faith and help him understand what was happening.

He reminded the homeless man of the prayer he had prayed, "Oh G-D, I can't do this anymore. I need You—I give up trying to do this on my own. I need You more than the food I need to eat. I need You more than the water I need to drink. I need You more than this stagnant city air I am breathing. Take me home. Life is just too hard! I can't do this anymore."

The Master continued talking with the man and told him, "This can be your home—this can be your life from now on." The homeless man was escorted to a bathroom and encouraged to shower. There was a fresh set of clothes waiting for him outside the shower. The Master then took him to a large closet full of clothes and told him that this and the contents within were now his. He showed the man the bedroom where he would sleep.

The homeless man lived with the Master for several months, learning the way of his Lord. Then the Master beckoned the homeless man to come closer. He smiled at him and embraced the man and then as He pulled away He said, "I believe you are ready now. You are strong enough to go back out into the world. Your assignment is to find the desperate, the hurting, those who are ready to give up everything to follow Me. Go to the byways and the highways inviting them to come. But don't stay out in the world too long—I don't want you to succumb to the world, your fleshly desires, and the devil. My home is your home now. I love you—I am your heavenly Father."

This allegorical vision was so real to me. I was moved to tears as I beheld this God-inspired parable. As I pondered this vision, I sensed that many of us do not understand what Yeshua did on the cross for us. He broke down the middle partition, the veil, separating us from access to G-D the Father in the heavenly holy of holies. After many of us come to know Yeshua as Messiah and Lord (Adonai), we look upon that as a one-time encounter. As years go by, we lose the understanding that the "born-again experience" wasn't meant to be a one-time event, but rather, it was our entranceway into an ongoing intimacy with the one true G-D of Israel.

Even though some of us enter into a deeper relationship with G-D through the person of the Holy Spirit and through communion with Yeshua, many times we partition our lives between our fellowships, Bible studies, or worship services and our ongoing day-to-day lives. For the most part we put spiritual things aside to attend to our worldly affairs. Of course, when we face bad circumstances, conflicts, opposition, sickness, and life's adversities, we become like the homeless man beseeching the Lord's intervention. We don't realize it, but we are living from crisis to crisis—from one need to another— because our moment-by-moment journey is lived separated from the One who wants to provide the very best for us—YHWH (YeHoVaH, YaHWeH, our heavenly Father).

The parable points to why this first portion of the Priestly Prayer of the Blessing is the most important thing you need to grasp in order to receive the full impartation of what G-D desires to give you. Your heavenly Father wants to make Himself available to you, not just to give you help as you seek His hand of salvation, deliverance, healing, or provision. But He, through this prayer—the greatest prayer of grace authored by Him—is making Himself available to you throughout each moment of your day.

"To bless" in the Hebrew means that He has left His heavenly abode and wants to kneel in front of you, making Himself available to you. Not just for you to receive the good things, which He desires to give you, but He kneels in front of you as an invitation for you to be with Him. He wants to place His name (*shem*) upon you. YHWH wants to supernaturally place a portion of His very person, His holy character, and His power and authority upon you. He is right in front of you, but it is up to you to respond to His presence by faith.

## ACCEPTING THIS PORTION OF THE PRAYER

Again I say, this first part of the Priestly Prayer of the Blessing is so important because if you do not understand and receive the truth of this reality, you will not access the rest of what He is about to impart to you through this divine prayer.

I remember one woman who received as a gift the framable print containing my amplified Hebrew-to-English translation of the prayer. She could not accept the actual translation of this first portion of the Priestly Prayer of the Blessing. Because she stumbled in receiving this first potion, she rejected the entire translation. I felt bad that she missed this life-changing invitation to know her heavenly Father in the most intimate and tangible way possible.

This first portion is the key to receiving the fullness of what will be imparted to us! She could not accept the fact that YHWH will bless her by kneeling down in front of her, making Himself available. She had been brought up as a Catholic and felt that the translation of the word *blessing* (as *barakh*) sounded blasphemous. She said, "How could the one true G-D who is so holy ever do such a thing?"

As I contemplated her reaction, I realized that I too was uncomfortable with it. While writing this book, I went on a trip to Israel as part of my role as a TV producer for Sid Roth's *It's Supernatural!*

TV program. There's something about being in the Holy Land. As I was praying about this first portion of G-D's divine prayer, the Lord placed the following thought in my mind.

I was confronted with the fact that Yeshua was one with the Father. He said that everything He does is what the Father had shown Him to do.

> Then [Yeshua] said to them, "Truly, truly I say to you, the Son can do nothing of Himself, but what He sees the Father do. For whatever He does, likewise the Son does."
>
> —JOHN 5:19

Everything Yeshua said is what the Father told Him to say.

> For I have not spoken on My own authority, but the Father who sent Me gave Me a command, what I should say and what I should speak.
>
> —JOHN 12:49

When asked by His disciples to reveal the heavenly Father to them, Yeshua shared that He is one with the Father and the Father is one with Him.

> Philip said to Him, "Lord, show us the Father, and that is sufficient for us."
>
> [Yeshua] said to him, "Have I been with you such a long time, and yet you have not known Me, Philip? He who has seen Me has seen the Father. So how can you say, 'Show us the Father'?"
>
> —JOHN 14:8–9

Many theologians convey that Yeshua came as YHWH (the heavenly Father) in the form of a man, as G-D's only begotten Son. In this way Yeshua demonstrated the Father's desire to save us, deliver us, heal us, and bless us. One scripture that identifies Yeshua's role to be the outward manifestation of YHWH (our heavenly Father) on earth is found in Paul's letter to the Colossians.

> For in Him [Yeshua] lives all the fullness of the Godhead [the Elohim, or the triune nature] bodily.
>
> —COLOSSIANS 2:9

The Amplified Bible conveys it this way:

For in Him all the fullness of Deity (the Godhead) dwells in bodily form [completely expressing the divine essence of {G-D}].

—COLOSSIANS 2:9, AMP

In other words, Yeshua was the *tangible evidence* of the invisible person of the Father and the Holy Spirit, clothed in bodily form so humanity might get to know the one true G-D of Israel.

## THE LAST SUPPER REVEALS THE MEANING OF *BARAKH*

We see the deeper meaning of the Hebrew word *barakh* through what Yeshua did during His final Passover Seder with His disciples.

[Yeshua], knowing that the Father had given all things into His hands and that He came from G-D and was going to G-D, rose from supper, laid aside His garments, and took a towel and wrapped Himself. After that, He poured water into a basin and began to wash the disciples' feet and to wipe them with the towel with which He was wrapped.

—JOHN 13:3–5

Yeshua, who is representing G-D the Father in the form of His only begotten Son, is on His knees washing the feet of the disciples. This is a perfect picture of *barakh* (to bless) being illustrated through Yeshua kneeling down in front of another. It appears that the disciples felt uncomfortable with this. They must of have been thinking that this was beneath the Messiah's dignity. He shouldn't be kneeling down in front of them washing their feet; instead they should be doing this for Him.

Peter was known for being outspoken:

Then He came to Simon Peter, and Peter said to Him, "Lord, are You washing my feet?"

[Yeshua] answered him, "You do not understand what I am doing now. But later you will understand."

Peter said to Him, "You shall never wash my feet!"

[Yeshua] answered him, "If I do not wash you, you have no part with Me."

Simon Peter said to Him, "Lord, not my feet only, but also my hands and my head!"

—JOHN 13:6–9

Yeshua desired to teach Peter and the other disciples how to bless others by being a servant. The Messiah explained that if Peter wouldn't allow Yeshua to bless him by washing his feet, then Peter could not have any true relationship with Yeshua. Peter suddenly changed his mind concerning Yeshua kneeling before him and responded, "Then don't just wash my feet, but give my whole body a bath!"

The Priestly Prayer of the Blessing is a prayer that the one true G-D has written and it has been given to us in order to have His very person imparted to us in the most intimate way possible. Having His name (*shem*) placed upon us is the way for us to begin to experience the Father supernaturally here on earth, as someday we will do forever in heaven.

Yeshua was demonstrating that YHWH's intention in this Priestly Prayer of the Blessing is, "I want to bless you. I want to kneel down in front of you, My son or My daughter, and make Myself available to you and by your receiving Me, you will receive all I have for you!"

## CONNECTING WITH YHWH LIKE NEVER BEFORE

Many believers have a personal relationship with Yeshua and the Holy Spirit. Many have by faith received Yeshua as their Messiah and Lord (Adonai), and through repentance and a simple prayer of salvation have begun to supernaturally experience the presence of Yeshua in their lives. Others have received a deeper, experiential, and supernatural relationship with the Ruach HaKodesh (Holy Spirit) through an encounter with Him. Some refer to this event as the "Baptism of the Holy Spirit," while others call it an awakening, revival, or renewal.

Yet it has been difficult for many of us to relate to YHWH our heavenly Father in an intimate and experiential way.

There has been unlimited teaching concerning "the Father heart of G-D." This teaching conveys that Yeshua showed us who the Father truly is by doing what the Father would have Him do. The Father was living through His only begotten Son, implementing everything His Son did and living vicariously through all that Yeshua experienced, even at the hands of His enemies.

Through religion we often view YHWH (our heavenly Father) as seated on His throne in heaven, holy, unapproachable, and surrounded by twenty-four elders and myriad angels on their faces worshipping Him. Though it is true that He is seated on His throne in heaven, holy and being worshipped continually, this divine prayer, which He alone authored, is the way in which YHWH helps us connect with Him in a supernatural, intimate, and experiential way like never before.

This Priestly Prayer of the Blessing was given for the children of Israel, but the Father now has revealed its relevance for every believer today! He has divulged how it can be proclaimed over us every day in a manner He intended. The main reason it was given is so that we can have His very person, His holy character, and His power and authority placed upon us.

Once we embrace Him and He embraces us, all the promises and gifts He wants to bestow upon us are imparted to us as a result of having Him with us in our lives in a very real way. Not only can we have intimacy with Yeshua and the Ruach HaKodesh, but now we can also have full access in a supernatural way to YHWH our heavenly Father.

This is the way to begin a relationship with what I call the fullness of the *Elohim* (the Godhead, the Trinity, the three-in-one)! The church has long been operating in a "two-cord relationship," but a "three-cord relationship" is now being made available through G-D's divine prayer. The Bible describes the importance of this three-cord relationship:

> This is the case of a man who is all alone, without a child or a brother, yet who works hard to gain as much wealth as he can. But then he asks himself, "Who am I working for? Why am I giving up so much pleasure now?" It is all so meaningless and depressing. Two people are better off than one, for they can help each other succeed. If one person falls, the other can reach out and help. But someone who falls alone is in real trouble. Likewise, two people lying close together can keep each other warm. But how can one be warm alone? A person standing alone can be attacked and defeated, but two can stand back-to-back and conquer. *Three are even better, for a triple-braided cord is not easily broken.*
> —ECCLESIASTES 4:8–12, NLT

I keep hearing from many men and women of G-D that there is a great move of G-D coming to invade planet Earth. They say it will not be like any other revival that occurred before! As a student of revivals I couldn't imagine how this next great end-time revival could be different from any other! Most moves are similar to ones that have occurred before. But I believe the Lord has shown me that the difference of this next revival will be in YHWH (our heavenly Father) revealing Himself in a way like never before—in the manifestation of the fullness of the Shekinah glory. For those of us who enter in, we will be walking in a far greater outpouring of the supernatural power of G-D. Yeshua said we will do "greater works [or miracles]" than He did (John 14:12). This will happen as a result of our walking in the fullness of the Elohim (the Father, Son, and Holy Spirit).

We now have only touched the surface of what the full implications are concerning this first portion of the Priestly Prayer of the Blessing. It is so important to grasp this truth, I feel compelled to go deeper to reveal what the Ruach HaKodesh downloaded to me concerning this first part of YHWH's divine prayer.

## DEEPER INSIGHT OF THE MEANING OF *BARAKH*

We know that many countries are led by dictators. If approached, these rulers require their subjects to follow special protocols and customs, such as bringing gifts and offerings, and to be sure to approach the ruler with humility, honor, and respectfulness. In olden times the king often sat upon his throne. The subject would enter his courts tentatively because of the authority and majesty of the king! Depending on the king's mood, your request might be granted or your life might be taken! Because it was so risky and unpredictable, most subjects in the kingdom would avoid approaching their king.

Religion often places separation, or distance, between G-D and us. It portrays YHWH (our heavenly Father) as seated on His throne in heaven, too holy to be approached. The truth is, the one true G-D of Israel, King of the universe, loves His spiritual sons and daughters and desires to come down from His throne in heaven, making Himself available to us in a tangible way. We often forget that He is omnipresent, meaning that He has the ability to be present everywhere at all times. In the Holy Scriptures there are a number of times when YHWH (the heavenly Father) Himself left His heavenly throne and came to reveal Himself to an undeserving people!

## YHWH VISITS THE EARTH IN CREATION

From the beginning, when Adam was created, we read that the Ruach HaKodesh moved upon the surface of the earth. The Hebrew word for G-D in Genesis chapter one is *Elohim*. It is a plural word for G-D; the triune nature of G-D is alluded to in creation: the Father, Son, and Holy Spirit.

> The earth was formless and void, darkness was over the surface of the deep, and the Spirit of G-D was moving over the surface of the water.
>
> —Genesis 1:2

It was as if the Ruach HaKodesh acted on behalf of G-D the Father's very hands in the act of creation. We read that G-D the Father speaks to the Son and the Holy Spirit that He wants to create the first man in their image and likeness.

> Then God [Elohim] said, "Let Us make man in Our image, after Our likeness…"
>
> —Genesis 1:26

We know that Adam—the first man—was fashioned out of the clay of the earth. But we read that it was YHWH the Father Himself that left His heavenly throne to come upon the earth to somehow kneel above Adam, who was in an inanimate form, made out of earthly clay.

> Then the Lord [G-D] formed man from the dust of the ground and breathed into his nostrils the breath of life, and man became a living being.
>
> —Genesis 2:7

The English words *Lord G-D* actually in the Hebrew are YHWH (YeHoVaH, or YaHWeH, the heavenly Father) Elohim. The Father had lowered His face to Adam's face and exhaled His breath into Adam's nostrils. Remember, the Hebrew word for breath is *NaShem*, and the Hebrew word for name is *shem*. Shem means more than the English word *name*. It means His very person, His holy character, and His power and authority. In essence YHWH breathed His DNA—His *shem* (His image and likeness) into an inanimate form of clay, and Adam came alive and transformed into the first human being.

Adam was filled with the Father's *shem*—His DNA, His glory, His life force, the very person of YHWH, the holy character of YHWH, and the power and authority of YHWH. Adam, though naked, was even clothed with the glory. Eve too, fashioned by G-D from the rib of Adam, received the *shem* of YHWH. Though she too was naked, she had the "supernatural clothes" of the glory of the Father.

We read in Genesis that YHWH would come down from His heavenly throne to bless Adam and Eve, and even did so when they disobeyed Him and ate fruit from the forbidden tree.

> Then they heard the sound of the LORD [G-D] walking in the garden in the cool of the day, and the man and his wife hid themselves from the presence of the LORD [G-D] among the trees of the garden.
>
> —GENESIS 3:8

## RESTORING THE RELATIONSHIP

Since the time Adam and Eve sinned and were expelled from the Garden of Eden, the desire of YHWH (our heavenly Father) has been to reestablish intimacy with mankind. He had created Adam and Eve in His likeness and image so He could have fellowship with someone of His own kind. He wanted a family of His own—sons and daughters!

The Bible indicates that YHWH understood loneliness. When He created the animals, He made both male and female. Each species had another who was created in their image and likeness so they would not be alone. Then once He created Adam, the heavenly Father said to him, "It is not good that you be alone!" (See Genesis 2:8.) YHWH's very reason for creating Adam was to have a son who would understand the heart of G-D and would be able to love and receive love back. G-D wanted to lavish blessings on Adam. But G-D knew that it wasn't good for Adam to be alone. So G-D created Eve out of the DNA of Adam's rib so Adam too would have someone created in his image and likeness.

The death both Adam and Eve suffered after they sinned was not a physical death; they lost free access to the intimacy they enjoyed in the Garden of Eden with their Father. No longer could they or their descendants see the face of G-D. The stain of original sin separated mankind from Him.

We all carry this empty hole within us. Something is definitely missing. We try and fill this loneliness and emptiness with substitutes for the real thing. It is our human spirit yearning for the missing relationship of communion with our heavenly Father.

Moses was allowed to get close again to YHWH his heavenly Father. He could hear His voice clearly and talk to Him as if face-to-face. G-D came down from heaven in the form of the Shekinah glory hidden in a cloud. Moses sensed His presence. There is nothing like being in the presence of G-D.

I will never forget my dream as a five-year-old boy where I encountered G-D in the form of the Shekinah glory in heaven; it changed my life! That one moment in time launched me into a search for the one true G-D. Being in His presence, to be touched by His glory, and hear His comforting voice—nothing else has ever been as powerful in my life. Forever the vision and experience of this I will always remember in vivid detail. I can still recall the wellness of being that flooded my person. The glory light, which was YHWH (the heavenly Father) Himself, was a golden bright light with colorful beams that fanned out toward me and all around me. These celestial beams of light formed a pathway leading to the source in the distance. All the time, I was being drawn closer to the light of the glory, close to the actual person of G-D the heavenly Father!

The main reason for your heavenly Father to kneel in front of you is so you can experience His divine embrace. He desires to impart Himself to you! As a result, all the good things He is and has for you will be transferred to you—His gifts and a portion of His inheritance for you, so you can fulfill your God-given destiny and purpose while on earth.

I say that those people who might challenge my amplified Hebrew-to-English translation of the first portion of the Priestly Prayer of the Blessing need to know that it must be understood and accepted in order for you to receive its full impartation.

In the Modern English Version this prayer begins with:

> The LORD bless you...
>
> —NUMBERS 6:24

But the amplified Hebrew-to-English translation I've created says:

May YHWH (He who exists) kneel before you (making Himself available to you as your heavenly Father) so He can grant, or bestow upon you His promises and gifts!

—NUMBERS 6:24

## THE ULTIMATE DOORWAY

*Barakh* communicates that we are to humble ourselves and bow in submission to G-D and offer to Him all we are and all we have. We are to give to Him our very person—every fiber of our being, every talent, everything He has given us—and show forth our appreciation for who He is. In this way we honor Him and lavish Him with gifts of praise and worship!

But what does it mean when it says that YHWH wants to bless us? Is it hard to accept the fact that the one true G-D of heaven and earth, YHWH, leaves His heavenly throne in some cosmic fashion to kneel before us to offer Himself to us? If we are honest, we would be like Peter was when Yeshua began to wash his feet, "I am not worthy!"

But this *first portion* of the Priestly Prayer of the Blessing is the most significant part of the prayer—it is the ultimate doorway to receive all the gifts and promises from heaven! G-D is making Himself available to you! Is it too hard to accept this unmerited favor? Not only did YHWH leave His throne in heaven during creation, but He did so many other times.

### YHWH in the burning bush

Not only does sin separate us from G-D and G-D from us, so does religion. Religion promulgates that G-D is far too holy for us to draw near. But Moses provides a different story.

Moses was allowed to draw near to G-D as He appeared in the burning bush. Moses clearly heard YHWH's voice. Moses was afraid. He could sense the holiness, and he was told to remove his sandals in reverence. His fear was so great he stammered when he answered G-D. When YHWH talked to Moses, he could hear G-D audibly and clearly.

Some religious scholars both in Judaism and Christianity say that it wasn't G-D Himself who appeared in the burning bush. They cannot accept that the holy G-D of Israel could leave His heavenly throne. Though they know He is omnipresent, they cannot fathom Him appearing in such a form as in the burning bush. These scholars say it was the "angel of the Lord" as mentioned in Exodus 3:2. The word *angel* in the Bible can also mean "messenger." Whether G-D had an intermediary or not, the language contained in this account makes it clear that G-D Himself had left His throne in heaven to communicate directly to Moses.

> The angel of [YHWH] appeared to him in a flame of fire from the midst of a bush, and he looked, and the bush burned with fire, but the bush was not consumed. So Moses said, "I will now turn aside and see this great sight, why the bush is not burnt."
>
> When [YHWH] saw that he turned aside to see, [G-D] called to him from out of the midst of the bush and said, "Moses, Moses." And he said, "Here am I."
>
> —Exodus 3:2–4

Can you see how YHWH directly communicated with Moses from the midst of the burning bush?

> [YHWH] said, "Do not approach here. Remove your sandals from off your feet, for the place on which you are standing is holy ground." Moreover He said, "I am the [Elohim] of your father, the [G-D] of Abraham, the [G-D] of Isaac, and the [G-D] of Jacob." And Moses hid his face, for he was afraid to look upon [G-D].
>
> —Exodus 3:5–6

The scriptures above cannot be any clearer. Moses's impression was that it was the G-D of Israel Himself who was being revealed in the burning bush. YHWH allowed Moses and the children of Israel to hear His voice!

Then on Mount Sinai after Moses led the children of Israel out of Egypt, as he stood in YHWH's Shekinah glory cloud and sensed YHWH's awesome presence, he again heard His voice. This was YHWH coming down to earth from His heavenly throne to bless Moses and the children of Israel. Moses received the Ten Commandments written by YHWH's own finger. It was YHWH's intent to come down from His high abode in heaven and bless those in covenant relationship with Him.

### YHWH in the glory cloud

The children of Israel had a lack of knowledge about who the G-D of Israel was when they were slaves in Egypt. They didn't have the

Word of YHWH—the Torah had not yet been given to them yet. Most of what they knew about G-D was passed down orally. They were frightened of YHWH. They had witnessed His awesome power as He sent ten plagues upon Egypt and placed judgment upon Israel's enemy, the pharaoh of Egypt.

When the children of Israel saw YHWH in the supernatural display of lightning on Mount Sinai and heard His voice that sounded like thunder, they told Moses they were too afraid. They would rather Moses go up and meet with G-D alone and then tell them what He was communicating.

> All the people witnessed the thunder and the lightning and the sound of the trumpet and the mountain smoking; and when the people saw it, they trembled and stood at a distance. They said to Moses, "You speak to us, and we will listen, but do not let [G-D] speak to us, lest we die."
>
> Moses said to the people, "Do not fear, for [G-D] has come to test you, so that the fear of Him may be before you so that you do not sin."
>
> The people stood a distance away as Moses drew near to the thick darkness where [G-D] was.
>
> —Exodus 20:18–21

Even the reflection of G-D's glory on the face of Moses was too much for the children of Israel to gaze upon as they watched Moses descend from the mountain to speak to them. They beseeched Moses to put a veil on his face. Yet it was only the reflection of YHWH's glory on Moses's face that made them afraid.

> When Moses came down from Mount Sinai with the two tablets of testimony in the hands of Moses, when he came down from the mountain, Moses did not know that the skin of his face shone while he talked with Him. So when Aaron and all the children of Israel saw Moses, amazingly, the skin of his face shone, and they were afraid to come near him. But Moses called to them, and Aaron and all the rulers of the congregation returned to him, and Moses spoke to them. Afterward all the children of Israel drew near, and he commanded them all that [YHWH] had spoken to him on Mount Sinai.
>
> When Moses finished speaking with them, he put a veil over his face. But whenever Moses went in before [YHWH] to speak

with Him, he took the veil off until he came out. Then he came out and spoke to the children of Israel what he had been commanded. The children of Israel saw the face of Moses, that the skin of Moses' face shone, and then Moses put the veil over his face again until he went in to speak with Him.

—Exodus 34:29–35

### YHWH in the tent of meeting

I have already shared about Moses's encounter with G-D in the Shekinah glory, before G-D had Moses build the tabernacle in the wilderness. While in the tent of meeting YHWH would come in the form of the Shekinah glory and meet with Moses. One time Joshua joined him too! Moses left the tent to attend to business, but Joshua stayed in the presence. It was not Moses who led the children of Israel into the Promised Land across the Jordan River, but Joshua.

The Shekinah glory is not a thing—it is the manifestation of YHWH (our heavenly Father). Remember when Moses asked YHWH, "Show me Your glory!" Moses wanted to see beyond the cloud. He wanted to see the source of the light that filled the tent. G-D said, "You cannot see *My face.*"

It was YHWH who equated the light in the midst of the glory cloud as being His very face! You can't get any more intimate with a person than when you are face-to-face with them!

But YHWH said to Moses, "No man can see My face." The best He could do with Moses was to tell him to cover his eyes as He passed before him. Then He set Moses on a rock in the secret place of the Most High G-D.

Then YHWH told Moses he would have an angel lead him into the Promised Land. But Moses objected. He didn't want an angel—a substitute for the person of YHWH. Moses said, "Unless You lead us, I won't go!"

In other words, Moses didn't want a substitute for the real presence of the person of G-D the Father. The closer Moses came to YHWH and spent time with Him, the more he wanted! When there was a problem and the children of Israel complained to Moses, he would go into the tent of meeting to hear from G-D. Moses went into the presence of the glory cloud and asked the heavenly Father for help.

## REMOVING THE SEPARATION

Religion wants to keep our heavenly Father away from our access, because the theologians believe we aren't worthy to be in His presence. Many Christian theologians stress that we can have an intimate relationship with Yeshua and the Ruach HaKodesh, but many in leadership still place encumbrances between us and our access to the Father.

Religion says that it is better to approach G-D through intermediaries such as a priest, pastor, or rabbi or special emissaries comprised of saints who have died and are now in heaven. We are told we must bring offerings (not bulls and goats, but financial offerings) and perform acts of penance in order to gain G-D's favor. But no matter what we do, religion never allows us to get closer because religion raises fences and encumbrances that hinder us from direct access. Religion tells us YHWH is unapproachable! He is on His throne in heaven and is far too holy for us to approach.

The tragedy is that Yeshua paid a brutal price on the cross that we might have direct access to the heavenly Father.

> For [Yeshua] is our peace, who has made both groups one and has broken down the barrier of *the dividing wall*.
>
> —EPHESIANS 2:14

The "dividing wall" refers to the ordinances under the old covenant that separated the children of Israel from the nations and also separated them from YHWH, who dwelt in the holy of holies in the form of the Shekinah glory. The "dividing wall" is typified by the veil in the tabernacle and later in the holy temple, which divided the holy place from the holy of holies.

When Yeshua was on the cross, He cried out, "It is finished!" and then He said, "Father, into Your hands I commit My spirit" (Luke 23:46). He breathed His last breath and died. The veil in the holy temple was rent in two from top to bottom. Theologians say it symbolizes the breaking down of the "dividing wall" of separation, granting every believer in Yeshua access to the heavenly holy of holies.

> Therefore, brothers, we have confidence to enter the Most Holy Place by the blood of Jesus, by a new and living way that He has opened for us through the veil, that is to say, His flesh.
>
> —HEBREWS 10:19–20

Theologians state that Yeshua's body being torn by the nails of the cross caused the veil to be torn so that we who believe in Yeshua as our Messiah and Lord now have access by faith to YHWH (our heavenly Father) in the heavenly throne room.

But I also believe that the veil was torn to indicate that YHWH can now come out to meet with His spiritual sons and daughters. Sin separated the heavenly Father from mankind because all of us were marked with the stain of "original sin." But Yeshua dealt with sin on the cross through His death as the "Lamb of [G-D], who takes away the sin of the world" (John 1:29). The Bible says concerning those of us who are under the new covenant:

> [YHWH] made [Yeshua] who knew no sin to be sin for us, that
> we might become the righteousness of [G-D] in Him.
> —2 CORINTHIANS 5:21

This means that now YHWH (our heavenly Father) can also come down to earth from His holy of holies in heaven, and approach His spiritual sons and daughters through His Priestly Prayer of the Blessing. Why? Because we who accept Yeshua have been made holy through the blood sacrifice of Yeshua.

Are you beginning to comprehend how G-D truly has reached out to make a way for intimacy with humanity time and time again? The most remarkable thing YHWH did was to come down from His heavenly throne to earth, making Himself known in a bodily form through Yeshua, His only begotten Son.

When one would look into the face of Yeshua, he would be beholding the face of the heavenly Father in a palatable form. G-D told Moses, who desired intimacy with Him, that he could not see the face of YHWH or he would surely die. But when a person looked at the face of Yeshua, they were peering into the face of YHWH, and instead of dying, they received life everlasting!

The Hebrew word barakh implies the ultimate gift of the coming of YHWH (our heavenly Father) from His heavenly throne onto the earth and making Himself available to us in the form of Yeshua the Messiah Himself. Yeshua said, "I am the way, the truth, and the life. No one comes to the Father except through Me" (John 14:6).

## YHWH in the New Jerusalem

Yeshua was the ultimate way in which YHWH (our heavenly Father) would make Himself available to us—until He comes to earth along with Yeshua in fulfillment of the prophecy in Revelation 21. Many talk about the second coming of Yeshua, but Yeshua isn't the only One coming back to earth when the New Jerusalem comes down from heaven.

> I saw no temple in the city, for the Lord [G-D Almighty, the Father] and the Lamb [Yeshua] are its temple. The city has no need of the sun or moon to shine in it, for the glory of [G-D, YHWH, our heavenly Father] is its light, and its lamp [the menorah, the lampstand] is the Lamb. And the nations of those who are saved shall walk in its light, and the kings of the earth shall bring their glory and honor into it. Its gates shall never be shut by day, for there shall be no night there. They shall bring into it the glory and the honor of the nations. No unclean thing shall ever enter it, nor shall anyone who commits abomination or falsehood, but only those whose names are written in the Lamb's Book of Life.
>
> —REVELATION 21:22–27

Can you understand how this first portion of the Priestly Prayer of the Blessing can become a stumbling block to some? The people who struggle with this first part of the amplified Hebrew-to-English translation must understand that YHWH, though holy and unapproachable, has continually reached out to embrace us with a desire to save us, redeem us, deliver us, heal us, and adopt us as His spiritual sons and daughters.

> For [G-D the Father] so loved the world that He gave His only *begotten Son*, that whoever believes in Him should not perish, but have eternal life.
>
> —JOHN 3:16

What does it mean that Yeshua was G-D's only *begotten* Son? Adam (first man) was YHWH's created son. It was YHWH's intention to create man in His likeness and image. How did He do this with Adam? He created Adam out of the clay of the earth. He then breathed into Adam's nostrils and imparted His DNA, His very breath, His holy character, and His power and authority.

The difference between Adam and Yeshua is that Adam was created and Yeshua was *begotten*. *Begotten* means YHWH actually sent His pure and holy seed into the womb of Miriam (Mary) and impregnated her. By Yeshua having the holy blood of YHWH, He was born without the stain of Adam's original sin. Adam had no mother, but he had YHWH as his Father, who created him and then breathed His life into him. On the other hand, Yeshua (Jesus) was YHWH's physical Son, created by His own seed planted in Miriam's womb. Which do you think was harder? The heavenly Father breathing His breath into Adam's nostrils or planting His holy seed into the womb of Miriam? Nothing is impossible for the one true G-D of Israel, the Creator of the universe!

When Yeshua took the beatings and the thirty-nine stripes from the Roman whip called the cat-o'-nine-tails, He did so to take your sickness upon Himself. But it wasn't only the Messiah who took this beating for you; it was YHWH (your heavenly Father) too!

The rabbinical extra-biblical writings talk about how YHWH actually can sense the pain, sickness, and sorrows that we as His people are facing. It is surmised that if He allowed one tear to fall from His eye, the entire earth would be flooded. These writings convey in a powerful way that YHWH has empathy for us.

> When [G-D] remembers His children [Israel], who dwell in misery among the nations, He lets fall two tears into the ocean, and the sound is heard from one end of the world to the other. So too when [G-D] remembers how the *Shekinah* lies in the dust of the earth, does He shed tears hot as fire, that fall down into the Great Sea.
>
> Others say that in the hour that [G-D] cries, five rivers of tears issue from the five fingers of His right hand, and fall into the Great Sea and shake the world.
>
> Many human characteristics are attributed to [G-D], even weeping. Here [G-D] weeps remembering the suffering of His children, Israel. Just as [G-D's] size is enormous…so too are [G-D's] tears.
>
> In *Esh Kadosh*, Rabbi Kalonymus Kalman Shapira proposes that the reason the world was not destroyed by [G-D's] suffering over the afflictions of Israel and the destruction of the temple is because [G-D] wept in secret, in His innermost chamber. For had His grief penetrated to this world, it would no longer exist.[1]

The implication here is that it wasn't only Yeshua who took your shame, your guilt, and your sin upon Himself as He hung on the cross—but YHWH (your heavenly Father) was vicariously suffering upon that cross through His only begotten Son. The holy blood that Yeshua was shedding for us on the cross was the very same blood of YHWH. The Torah states:

> For the life of the flesh is in the blood, and I have given it to you on the altar to make atonement for your lives; for it is the blood that makes atonement for the soul.
>
> —LEVITICUS 17:11

It was the holy blood of YHWH (our heavenly Father) that flowed through Yeshua's veins. G-D's sole seed was placed into the womb of Yeshua's mother, Miriam (Mary), in order to conceive the only begotten Son. Yeshua paid the price of your sin so you can become born again—an adopted son or daughter of the Most High G-D.

It was YHWH Himself who came in the form of His only begotten Son and vicariously suffered. YHWH (our heavenly Father) also was reviled by men and beaten. The Father could identify with His only begotten Son, Yeshua, whose arms were outstretched—held by the nails of crucifixion! Yeshua died a horrible death upon the cross. G-D the Father could sense every pain that His Son suffered for us in this brutal death sentence. In light of this how can we ever question whether YHWH (our heavenly Father) would kneel before us with outstretched hands, beckoning us to come to Him so He can enfold us with His divine embrace?

There is no good reason left to refuse to accept that through this first portion of the Priestly Prayer of the Blessing, YHWH (our heavenly Father) wants to come down from His heavenly throne to kneel before you, His son or daughter, to minister to you and to impart a portion of Himself to you! YHWH so loves you. He even came in the form of His only begotten Son to take the punishment you deserved and died in your place to take away your sin!

Do you see now why YHWH chose to write this portion as the first part of His divine prayer of the blessing? If you can grasp and receive this, then the fullness of impartation from the rest of the Priestly Prayer of the Blessing will become fully available to you!

## KEYS TO THE BLESSING

Why would G-D tell you in the Scriptures to seek His face if it wasn't possible for you to find it?

## STUDY QUESTIONS

Why is this first portion of the Priestly Prayer of the Blessing so important to understand and accept?

_____

_____

_____

What is your response supposed to be when YHWH kneels in front of you through this first portion of the divine prayer?

_____

_____

_____

Since Yeshua was YHWH who came in the form of His only begotten Son, what does Yeshua's kneeling before the disciples illustrate about your heavenly Father's heart?

_____

_____

_____

## PRAYER

*Heavenly Father, I am overwhelmed by the reality that You want to kneel in front of me with Your arms reaching out to me. I repent of my ignorance to the fact that You want me to recognize You and receive Your selfless love for me as Your spiritual child. By the power of the Ruach HaKodesh (Holy Spirit) I ask You to help me sense the reality of Your nearness and presence.*

*Daddy G-D, I declare my love for You. I want and need You in my life! Seal this moment and never let me forget it. Let it be the beginning of my pursuing an intimate, supernatural, and experiential relationship with You as my heavenly Father. I pray this in the name of Yeshua (Jesus).*

# Chapter 11

# THE HEBREW WORD FOR KEEP

## שָׁמַר

*Shamar*, "to hedge about with thorns"
(Hebrew is read from right to left)

T HE NEXT WORD in the Priestly Prayer of the Blessing is *keep*.

The LORD bless you and *keep* you...

—NUMBERS 6:24

The English word *keep* is abstract. The Hebrew word is *shamar* and its meaning is concrete. Most of us think of this word when it comes to keeping the commandments or the Word of G-D.

> Therefore, you shall *keep* His statutes [Sabbath and feasts] and His commandments [*mitzvot*, which means His directions for the way we are to walk so we don't get lost] which I command you this day, so that it may go well with you and with your children after you, and so that you may prolong your days [Hebraic concept of salvation, which includes health, prosperity, protection, provision and a long life] in the land, which the LORD your [G-D] gives you, forever.
>
> —DEUTERONOMY 4:40

The statutes and commandments of G-D are our directions to safely navigate through this life and also obtain the favor and blessings that YHWH has for us. But this Hebrew word *shamar* means so much more than the English word *keep*.

Most of us equate the word *keep* with obedience. In reality it carries the idea of guarding. A shepherd in the wilderness would build a corral to protect his sheep from predators. They would use stones to fashion a wall and then place thornbushes on top to keep out predators, such as wolves.

YHWH (our heavenly Father) is saying that He will place a

hedge of protection around us, hemming us in with thorns to keep the enemy (predators) from getting to us.

## SEE IT IN YOUR MIND'S EYE

In chapter 10 I dealt with the word *bless* and revealed the simple picture of YHWH kneeling before you as a good parent who would do anything for you, His spiritual child, desiring to demonstrate His availability to you. I shared with you that G-D your Father is actually making Himself available to you through this first portion of the divine prayer.

Should you and I ignore Him? Should we just stand and look at Him? No! We are moved to respond in our hearts and humble ourselves, and we fall to our knees so we can receive His invitation. Once we are kneeling with Him, we are positioned to receive His divine embrace. The one true G-D of Israel has come down from His heavenly throne to enfold us with His strong, loving arms.

The picture I present to you in this second portion of the divine prayer is that we are kneeling down (humbled) facing G-D our Father. When it says YHWH will "keep you," it is as if He now enfolds you in His arms with a divine embrace.

It is His arms that are likened to a "thorny hedge" of protection. Satan and his demons can never penetrate the security of the arms of YHWH. You are protected from all things. Why? Because G-D sees us as His spiritual sons and daughters because of what Yeshua (Jesus) did on the cross for us.

> For as many as are led by the Spirit of [G-D], these are the sons of [G-D]. For you have not received the spirit of slavery again to fear. But you received the Spirit of adoption, by whom we cry, "Abba, Father."
>
> —ROMANS 8:14–15

When YHWH (your heavenly Father) places His arms around you in His divine embrace, nothing can hurt you or separate you from Him.

> What then shall we say to these things? If [YHWH] is for us, who can be against us? He who did not spare His own Son, but delivered Him up for us all, how shall He not with Him also freely give us all things? Who shall bring a charge against [G-D's]

elect? It is [YHWH] who justifies. Who is he who condemns? It is Christ [the Messiah] who died, yes, who is risen, who is also at the right hand of [YHWH, G-D the Father], who also intercedes for us. Who shall separate us from the love of Christ [the Messiah]? Shall tribulation, or distress, or persecution, or famine, or nakedness, or peril, or sword?

—ROMANS 8:31–35

This is what the divine embrace of YHWH (our heavenly Father) brings: security, protection, and victory over the forces of the enemy!

No, in all these things we are more than conquerors through Him who loved us. For I am persuaded that neither death nor life, neither angels nor principalities nor powers, neither things present nor things to come, neither height nor depth, nor any other created thing, shall be able to separate us from the love of [YHWH, G-D our Father], which is in the [Messiah Yeshua] our [Adonai].

—ROMANS 8:37–39

Satan and his principalities and powers are committed to interfere with us and our God-given destiny and purpose! Satan hates YHWH more than any other entity. Above all, Satan doesn't want us to get anywhere close to G-D the Father, because the devil knows we will be given the power and authority to help set the spiritual captives free.

Satan will use other people to come against us. He may directly come against us himself by spiritually harassing us, oppressing us, and in some cases possessing us, if we haven't yet recognized Yeshua as our Messiah and our Lord.

With the divine embrace of our heavenly Father through this Priestly Prayer of the Blessing we are delivered *instantly* from the enemy's attacks, whether it be from others, or from spiritual harassment, oppression, and in some cases possession.

Many of us might have sought deliverance in the past only to find that we gain relief for a short time after the deliverance is performed. Yet most times these attacks begin again. It may not be the same area from which we were delivered before, but instead a new area of conflict, oppression, or harassment occurs. It is as if we are now continually consumed by a "cycle of unending deliverance" as a way of life.

> Rather [YHWH your Elohim] you shall fear, and He will deliver
> you from the hand of all your enemies.
>
> —2 KINGS 17:39

When we pursue "deliverance as a way of life," it is almost as if we are not seeking our heavenly Father and His presence, but instead, we are trying to identify the demonic spirit that is coming against us. YHWH loves you and honors your request when you seek deliverance. But the process sometimes seems never-ending. It might be that we are even empowering the demonic realm by believing that Satan has so much power over us.

Through this second portion of the Priestly Prayer of the Blessing when YHWH (your heavenly Father) comes and supernaturally places His arms around you in His divine embrace, you don't have to ask for deliverance—it is done instantly for you.

> The LORD is my pillar, and my fortress, and my *deliverer*; my
> [G-D], my rock, in whom I take refuge; my shield, and the horn
> of my salvation, my high tower.
>
> —PSALM 18:2

Again I point out that it is OK for you to seek an end to harassment and attacks of the enemy, or deliverance from demonic spirits. YHWH will honor those efforts. Better yet, if you allow the impartation of His name (*shem*) to come upon you through this Priestly Prayer of the Blessing, you receive Him (His very person, His holy character, and His power and authority). In this second portion of the divine prayer of the blessing, through G-D's divine embrace, *deliverance and protection* come without your asking. It is that simple! When you come into an understanding of the full revelation of what this Priestly Prayer of the Blessing is actually accomplishing and imputing to you, it will be life transforming!

## THE CONNECTION TO PSALM 91

One of the most well-known psalms about G-D's protection for His people is found in Psalm 91. There have been many books and sermons about this one particular chapter in the Tanakh (Old Testament). One great testimony book was written by Peggy Joyce Ruth entitled *Psalm 91: Real-Life Stories of God's Shield of Protection and What This Psalm Means for You and Those You Love.*

This book tells that Peggy's husband was in a private airplane when it crashed into the sea. He and several people along with the pilot were stuck floating in the frigid ocean, subject to sharks swimming near them. One after another, they began to perish.

Peggy's husband had studied and meditated on Psalm 91. He began to continually proclaim and believe by faith the words of this psalm. As a result, he attributed the powerful words of Psalm 91 as the reason he lived through this horrible ordeal and was rescued. Only he and the pilot survived. Even the secular news dubbed his survival as a *documented miracle*.[1]

I have always found the words contained in Psalm 91 to be anointed and filled with power to bring divine protection and keep us from harm. Yet ever since YHWH imparted to me the full revelation of the divine prayer and how to have it proclaimed over me in the name (*shem*) of Yeshua, I realized that the full impartation of Psalm 91 is related to this second portion of the prayer: "YHWH keep you." This is an impartation of G-D as our protector!

> He who dwells in the shelter of the Most High shall abide under the shadow of the Almighty.
>
> —PSALM 91:1

Now I will explain the key for receiving His divine protection, which is available for those who dwell (abide) under the shadow of "the Almighty." In Hebrew the words for the Almighty are *El Shaddai*. The high priest Aaron would hold both his hands up in the form of the Hebrew letter shin. This symbol stood for *El Shaddai—G-D Almighty*.

Therefore the scripture above makes it clear that you should make it your aim to abide in that secret place of YHWH (your heavenly Father). This isn't just an intellectual exercise, but in fact, YHWH makes Himself available to you, enfolding His strong arms around you—so that His shadow of protection covers you.

In order for the *shadow of another person* to be able to cover you, you must be very close to that person and the person must be big in order for his shadow to cover you. As we delve deeper into the connection between Psalm 91 and this second portion of the Priestly Prayer of the Blessing, we begin to understand the powerful revelation of what happens as our heavenly Father enfolds His arms around us in a divine embrace.

> I will say of the LORD, "He is my refuge and my fortress, my
> [G-D] in whom I trust."
>
> —PSALM 91:2

The Hebrew word for Lord is *Adonai*, but in the original Hebrew Scriptures, the name used in this verse is the sacred name of YHWH, that of YeHoVaH or YaHWeH. This is the sacred name of the Most High G-D of Israel, our heavenly Father.

The main point of Psalm 91:2 is that we confess Him as being our place of refuge, our fortress, and it's an admission that we have complete trust in Him. It is one thing to confess that He is your refuge and fortress, but this confession becomes reality when we actually realize that He is truly right in front of us. The Lord showed me how to understand how close His face wants to come to us.

Let me ask you to do something. Hold your hand closely in front of your face so you can focus on your palm. That is how close your heavenly Father wants to be with you! The protection fully comes as you allow Him to enfold you with His strong arms in a divine embrace.

> Surely He shall deliver you from the snare of the hunter and from
> the deadly pestilence.
>
> —PSALM 91:3

Here is a clear reference to the fact that in His arms, in His divine embrace, we will experience His deliverance from the hunter—or as some translations like the King James Version say, the *fowler.*

What is a *fowler?* This refers to people who hunt *fowl.* More specific than just being hunters, they are professional *bird* hunters. In the days before firearms, birds were captured through an interesting method in which the hunter would take young birds from a nest and raise them by hand. Then when they had become tame, they were confined in hidden cages so that their voices would call others of their kind, and then the arrows of concealed hunters (fowlers) could kill them.

This scripture refers to being protected from this particular tactic in which innocent, young, and impressionable people are entrapped by Satan himself "and raised by his hand." Their voices, or the very character of these people, attract others who are of like kind, meaning those who have their same faults or weaknesses. Those who are attracted are then picked off by *hunter demons,* which are ready to destroy and kill. In the divine embrace of our heavenly Father, we are protected because the enemy cannot come near us under His impenetrable protection.

Likewise, in the divine embrace of G-D, no pestilence can harm you because where YHWH is, there is no sickness! His kingdom is perfect because He is there, and through His divine embrace we are immersed in the atmosphere of heaven.

> He shall cover you with His feathers, and under His wings you shall find protection; His faithfulness shall be your shield and wall.
>
> —PSALM 91:4

This directly relates to G-D's arms embracing us like a mother bird to protect us and keep us safe. His faithfulness refers to His promises becoming our shield to deflect any attacks of the enemy's arrows.

> You shall not be afraid of the terror by night, nor of the arrow that flies by day; nor of the pestilence that pursues in darkness, nor of the destruction that strikes at noonday.
>
> —PSALM 91:5–6

This passage guarantees that even in times when we are in the darkness of the night, when there appears to be danger lurking, we can be reassured because of His divine embrace that we are not alone. He is with us, protecting us.

When we are going through our day, we do not have to be afraid that the enemy can be lurking and even stalking us to do harm. YHWH is surrounding us with His thorny arms of protection, which keep the predators from having access to us.

> A thousand may fall at your side and ten thousand at your right hand, but it shall not come near you.
>
> —PSALM 91:7

We may be witnessing the insanity of the world around us with people engaged in battle against one another. The danger of their warfare may bring casualties when we look to our right and left— very close to us—but He promises that His divine embrace will not allow this aimless violence to affect us.

> Only with your eyes shall you behold and see the reward of the wicked.
>
> —PSALM 91:8

The New Living Translation translates the above verse this way…

Just open your eyes, and see how the wicked are punished.

Being in His divine embrace, we are given eyes to see beyond the apparent prosperity of those who are wicked. We will be given insight to see things through YHWH's own eyes. We will be enabled to see what lies behind the exterior success of those who are wicked. We will no longer envy them because we will see the truth of the justice of G-D that will someday be enforced upon them. On the outside they may look happy, but those who live apart from Him are suffering and grieving on the inside! You can be sure of that!

> Because you have made the LORD, who is my refuge, even the Most High, your dwelling, there shall be no evil befall you, neither shall any plague come near your tent; for He shall give His angels charge over you to guard you in all your ways. They shall bear you up in their hands, lest you strike your foot against a stone.
>
> —PSALM 91:9–12

The above emphasizes that because we have the very name (*shem*) placed upon us, we are immune to plagues. We will have angels surrounding us to keep us protected wherever we are and wherever we go. These angels, assigned by YHWH Himself, bear us up so we are protected from accidentally hitting our foot on a stone.

> You shall tread upon the lion and adder; the young lion and the serpent you shall trample underfoot.
>
> —PSALM 91:13

When we are in His keeping, we will have victory over the predators that are lurking, watching us, waiting until they determine we are weak, ready to attack us at the time when we appear most vulnerable.

YHWH allows us to see them and where they are hiding. If we choose to go after them, we will be victorious! The lion symbolizes the strongest of our enemies; the adder (serpent) symbolizes those who are stealth, are sneaky, and have the ability to swiftly strike, inflicting a bite that injects us with poison, bringing a slow and painful death.

The serpent also represents Satan himself. Yeshua's victory on the cross treaded upon the serpent, and He has Satan's very head under His feet. So too we who are seated in heavenly places with Messiah have the ability to step on Satan and impair him from attacking.

> Because he has set his love upon Me, therefore I will deliver him;
> I will set him on high, because he has known My name.
>
> —PSALM 91:14

The above verse reminds us that all of the stated promises within Psalm 91 come about as a result of setting our hearts, minds, souls, spirits, and every fiber of our beings on loving the one true G-D of Israel and desiring that He will be first in our lives.

YHWH is telling us that all this is possible because we have known His name. The promised result of the Priestly Prayer of the Blessing being proclaimed over you is that He places His name upon you. His *shem* (His very person, His holy character, His power and authority) is imparted and placed upon you!

This means He delivers us and sets us high above the enemy and the things of this world. The enemy of our souls cannot harm us. The ultimate promise of YHWH (our heavenly Father) is proclaimed in His own words in the last two verses of Psalm 91:

> He shall call upon Me, and I will answer him; I will be with him
> in trouble, and I will deliver him and honor him. With long life I
> will satisfy him and show him My salvation.
>
> —PSALM 91:15–16

The full amplified Hebrew-to-English translation of this portion of the Priestly Prayer of the Blessing is far more than what we find in our Bibles. Our English Bibles say:

> The LORD bless you and *keep you*...
>
> —NUMBERS 6:24

But the amplified English-to-Hebrew translation is...

> May YHWH (YeHoVaH, YaHWeH, your heavenly Father) guard
> you with a hedge of thorny protection that will prevent Satan and
> all your enemies from harming you. May He protect your body,
> soul, mind, and spirit, your loved ones, and all your possessions!

When our Jewish High Priest, Yeshua, proclaims this portion of the Priestly Prayer of the Blessing upon you, YHWH (your heavenly Father) will appear before you and will give you His divine embrace.

## KEYS TO THE BLESSING

"To keep you" means YHWH is now giving you His divine embrace.

## STUDY QUESTIONS

What benefits do you receive when YHWH (your heavenly Father) places His arms around you in His divine embrace?

_____

_____

_____

Why do you not need to ask for deliverance when you are in His divine embrace?

_____

_____

_____

What are some of the promises of Psalm 91, which you receive by default in the divine embrace of YHWH?

_____

_____

_____

## Chapter 12

# THE HEBREW WORD FOR FACE

# פָּנִים

*Panim*, plural form, "entire being"
(Hebrew is read from right to left)

WE'VE DISCUSSED THE words *Lord, bless,* and *keep.* The next abstract word in the Priestly Prayer of the Blessing is *face.*

> The LORD bless you and keep you; the LORD make His *face*...
> —NUMBERS 6:24–25

The Hebrew word *panim* comes from the root *panah,* which means "to turn." The word *panim* is plural. It implies in Hebrew "more than one face." So, not just a happy face, but also a sad face, an angry face, and the entire being that is revealed in the face.

This means when we behold G-D's face, we can see Him as He truly is—fully divine, yet a person. When we see Him face-to-face we can observe that He has expressions that connote His emotions, thoughts, and judgments.

Religion tries to keep us from seeing our heavenly Father in these terms, keeping YHWH in a distant relationship. Religion advocates that G-D the Father remains too holy to approach; it is even taught that He is a mystery. We forget that G-D is a person—and the Scriptures are full of illustrations of this fact.

### YHWH gets angry.

> And the LORD was angry with Solomon because he turned his heart away from the LORD [G-D] of Israel, who had appeared to him twice, and had warned him about this, that he should not follow other gods, but he was disobedient to the LORD's command.
> —1 KINGS 11:9–10

## YHWH has wrath.

> The wrath of [G-D] is revealed from heaven against all ungodliness and unrighteousness of men, who hold the truth in unrighteousness.
>
> —ROMANS 1:18

## YHWH can hate.

> Those who boast will not stand in Your sight; You hate all workers of iniquity.
>
> —PSALM 5:5

I must say that I am very glad that I am saved and standing in the shadow of the Lord Yeshua (Jesus). G-D has a pure hate, but it is also a complete and just hate. I am so thankful that I do not have to face that hate!

## YHWH takes pleasure in people and things.

> For the LORD takes pleasure in His people; He will beautify the meek with salvation.
>
> —PSALM 149:4

## YHWH gets sad and grieves.

> The LORD saw that the wickedness of man was great on the earth, and that every intent of the thoughts of his heart was continually only evil. The LORD was sorry that He had made man on the earth, and it grieved Him in His heart.
>
> —GENESIS 6:5–6

## YHWH has pity.

> As a father pities his children, so the LORD pities those who fear him.
>
> —PSALM 103:13, NKJV

## YHWH has compassion.

> The LORD is gracious and full of compassion, slow to anger, and great in mercy.
>
> —PSALM 145:8

Compassion: What is compassion? Funk and Wagnall's tell us, "Pity for the suffering or distress of another, with the desire to help or spare."[1] Think of that! He is full of compassion. If you need any, He has it. He, the infinite in size, is full, infinitely full of compassion!

## YHWH can be jealous.

> You shall not bow down to them, nor serve them. For I, the LORD your [G-D], am a jealous [G-D], visiting the iniquity of the fathers on the children, and on the third and fourth generations of whose who hate Me.
>
> —DEUTERONOMY 5:9

So you see that YHWH (our heavenly Father) is a person. G-D sent His only begotten Son, Yeshua, to demonstrate how much He loves us—to demonstrate His holy character. Yeshua is the fullness of the Godhead—the *Elohim*—in bodily form for us to see.

> Beware lest anyone captivate you through philosophy and vain deceit, in the tradition of men and the elementary principles of the world, and not after [the Messiah]. For in [Yeshua, Jesus] lives all the fullness of the [Elohim] bodily. And you are [being made] complete in Him, who is the head of all authority and power [He has authority and power over all principalities].
>
> —COLOSSIANS 2:8–10

Everything Yeshua did is what G-D the Father told Him to do. When Yeshua came, it was G-D the Father in the form of a man— to show forth His character to us. He had given us His Word, but mankind didn't comprehend and implement G-D's instruction and precepts. G-D wanted us to know what He was truly like. The compassion to heal and deliver us is what G-D desired to demonstrate to us all along!

G-D the Father is a person, and He desires a relationship with us! He desires to fellowship and commune and exchange intimacy. That's why He went to such lengths pursuing us and sending Yeshua (His only begotten Son) to open the way for us to obtain intimacy! G-D desires a two-way relationship! The precepts and commandments He has given us in His Law (Torah) are perfect. Through His instruction and the commandments Yeshua shared and clarified, our heavenly Father gives us *the way* to have an intimate relationship with Him.

There are many scriptures in the Tanakh (Old Testament) where we are encouraged to seek the face of YHWH. It is our heavenly Father's desire to have communion with us. The very first commandment is, "Love the LORD your [G-D] with all your heart and mind and with all your soul and with all your strength [your entire being]" (Deut. 6:5, AMP; see also Matt. 22:37; Mark 12:30; Luke 10:27).

The encouragement to seek the face of YHWH (our heavenly Father) alludes to the importance of getting to know the G-D of Israel in the most intimate way.

> When You said, "Seek My face," my heart said to You, "Your face, LORD, I will seek."
>
> —PSALM 27:8

Yet, concerning this portion of the Priestly Prayer of the Blessing, though we are encouraged to seek His face, it is YHWH, our heavenly Father, who is making Himself available by showing His face to us.

## SEE IT IN YOUR MIND'S EYE

Remember the first portion of the Priestly Prayer of the Blessing? This dealt with the fact that YHWH wants to bless you.

> The LORD *bless you . . .*
>
> —NUMBERS 6:24

The simple picture of what YHWH is doing through that first portion of this prayer is, He is kneeling before you as a good parent who would do anything for you His child, desiring to demonstrate His availability to you. As a child seeing your Daddy kneeling in front of you with His arms extended inviting you, you are moved to respond and humble yourself, and you fall to your knees so you can receive His invitation.

I also shared with you about the second portion of the prayer. Once you are kneeling down (humbled) facing YHWH, He now enfolds you in His arms with His divine embrace.

> The LORD bless you and *keep you.*
>
> —NUMBERS 6:24

He embraces you in His arms that are likened to a "thorny hedge of protection." Satan and his demons can never penetrate the security of the arms of YHWH. You are protected from all things. When your heavenly Father places His arms around you with His divine embrace, nothing can hurt you or separate you from Him.

In the third portion of the Priestly Prayer of the Blessing, your heavenly Father now loosens His embrace. While still keeping His holy hands upon your shoulders, He pulls away so you can now see Him face-to-face.

> The LORD bless you and keep you; the LORD make His *face* to shine upon you...
> 
> —NUMBERS 6:24–25

I have already shared with you in chapter 4 that the Shekinah glory cloud hid the actual face of YHWH from Moses's view. In the Book of Exodus we read that Moses stopped going up onto Mount Sinai to meet with YHWH. Before the actual tabernacle was erected where YHWH would take up residence in the holy of holies in the form of the Shekinah glory, Moses fashioned a temporary dwelling place where he could meet with YHWH. (See Exodus 33:7–11.)

It was in that tent of meeting that YHWH came to dwell in the form of the Shekinah glory until the tabernacle in the wilderness was built. I must stress this point. Remember that the Shekinah glory is not just a thing, but a person, *the person of YHWH (our heavenly Father) Himself.*

I can't imagine what it felt like when Moses stood in the midst of the cloud of the Shekinah glory, which was the manifestation of the actual presence of the Father Himself. Moses could clearly hear YHWH's voice and spoke to Him as a man speaks to another man. Moses saw inside the cloud the bright light—the glory light—but the cloud obscured the source of the light.

I also already shared with you in an earlier chapter that Moses wanted to see beyond the glory cloud (vv. 18–20). Moses wanted to see the source of the light that was hidden by the cloud, which Moses referred to as the glory of G-D. But YHWH let Moses know that the glory light in the cloud was actually His very face (*panim*). It wasn't possible for Moses to see the *panim* of G-D clearly without the surrounding cloud that hid the full view. Anyone who beheld His face in that day would surely die.

Moses was still a man stained with the original sin of Adam. Moses had killed an Egyptian guard while in Egypt, and there wasn't yet established the sacrificial system under the Torah where sin and trespasses could be forgiven through the shedding of the blood of *kosher* (biblically cleaned or sanctioned) animals. The sacrificial system, which expounds about the way we can obtain grace and forgiveness, would soon be revealed by YHWH once He gave Moses the Torah and His plans on how to build the tabernacle in the wilderness.

## WHY DID MOSES WANT TO SEE THE FACE OF YHWH?

Talking to someone without seeing their face is good, but it is still distant communication. True intimacy comes when we can see another person face-to-face. When we look into the eyes of another, we can see their expression.

When we talk to another on the telephone, we are able to communicate, but we really can't discern fully what the other person truly feels about the things being discussed. Many say communication through emails or text messages is imperfect because people can't discern tone of voice or facial expressions to properly interpret the intricacies of what is truly being conveyed. When we can look upon the face of another person, their expression helps us better discern how they truly feel.

The statement that the eyes are the window of the soul has been attributed to everyone from Shakespeare to Da Vinci. The Bible says it this way.

> The light of the body is the eye. Therefore, if your eye is clear, your whole body will be full of light. But if your eye is unclear, your whole body will be full of darkness. Therefore, if the light that is in you is darkness, how great is that darkness!
> —MATTHEW 6:22–23

So far we have been talking about G-D's face spiritually being made available to us when we have become sons and daughters of the Most High G-D of Israel. This next verse of scripture communicates what it will be like when we can physically (not just spiritually) look into the face of YHWH (our heavenly Father).

For now we see as through a glass, dimly, but then, face to face.
Now I know in part, but then I shall know, even as I also am known.

—1 CORINTHIANS 13:12

YHWH communicated in the Tanakh (Old Testament) that we are to seek His face. This means if we truly love Him with all our heart, mind, soul, spirit, and strength, we would want to have the highest level of intimacy possible. King David valued this type of intimacy with YHWH.

Do not hide Your face from me in the day when I am in trouble;
incline Your ear to me; in the day when I call answer me quickly.

—PSALM 102:2

Jacob wrestled with the angel of the Lord, desiring that YHWH would bless him. When he received the blessing of having his name changed from Jacob to Israel (the father of the twelve sons who led the twelve tribes of Israel), he recognized that he had seen the very face (*panim*) of YHWH in the person of the angel of the Lord.

Jacob called the name of the place Peniel, saying, "I have seen [G-D] face to face, and my life has been preserved."

—GENESIS 32:30

Yeshua was the face of the Father when He was on earth. Even when we were still in our sinful state, to look at Jesus was to behold the very face of YHWH (our heavenly Father). Yet instead of bringing death, peering into the face of Yeshua brought us salvation and life everlasting! There is a powerful of example from the Scriptures concerning this truth.

One of the Pharisees asked [Yeshua, Jesus] to eat with him. So He went to the Pharisee's house and sat down for supper. There, a woman of the city who was a sinner, when she learned that [Yeshua] was sitting for supper in the Pharisee's house, brought an alabaster jar of ointment, and stood behind Him at His feet, weeping, and began to wash His feet with tears, and wiped them with the hair of her head, and kissed His feet, and anointed them with the ointment.

—LUKE 7:36–38

The inference here is that the woman was one of ill repute. Concerning the Jewish traditions of the time, a woman would never be allowed to touch a rabbi, let alone sit at his feet displaying such affection, especially a "woman of the city."

She had expensive alabaster oil, and may I point out that she didn't kneel in front of Him, but instead at first "stood behind Him." As time went on, she was most likely kneeling, stooping down, kissing Yeshua's feet, and anointing them with the oil. The fact that she wouldn't face Yeshua telegraphs that she was ashamed of her past sinful life.

> Now when the Pharisee who had invited Him saw it, he said to himself, "If this Man were a prophet, He would have known who and what kind of woman she is who is touching Him, for she is a sinner."
>
> —LUKE 7:39

Though this Pharisee muttered these words under his breath, Yeshua was able to hear his negative comment. Or perhaps, He even read the mind of the Pharisee?

> [Yeshua] answered him, "Simon, I have something to say to you."
> [The Pharisee] said, "Teacher, say it."
> "A creditor had two debtors. The one owed five hundred denarii, and the other fifty. When they had no money to pay, he freely forgave them both. Tell Me, therefore, which of them will love him more?"
> Simon answered, "I suppose he whom he forgave more."
> He said to him, "You have judged rightly."
>
> —LUKE 7:40–43

The point of Yeshua's parable was that He came to reach the brokenhearted—not the self-righteous—because they truly needed salvation, and as a result of receiving their miracle would begin to love G-D with all their heart, mind, soul, spirit, and strength.

> Then He turned to the woman and said to Simon, "Do you see this woman? I entered your house. You gave Me no water for My feet, but she has washed My feet with her tears and wiped them with the hair of her head. You gave Me no kiss, but this woman, since the time I came in, has not ceased to kiss My feet. You did not anoint My head with oil, but this woman has anointed My feet

with ointment. Therefore I say to you, her sins, which are many, are forgiven, for she loved much. But he who is forgiven little loves little."

—LUKE 7:44–47

Now the most important point of this account is related to seeing G-D face-to-face. This woman of ill repute was afraid to look up at the face of Yeshua, but truly she had been affected by hearing His words in the past, or possibly was moved by the miracles He had performed. She knew Yeshua was more than just another rabbi. There was something supernatural concerning Yeshua, who was full of compassion for sinners, the hurting, the sick, and even the demon possessed.

Yet the most significant portion of this account is what happened next. Yeshua turned to the woman and addressed her face-to-face. She looked into the eyes of Yeshua as He talked directly to her for the first time.

Then He said to her, "Your sins are forgiven."

—LUKE 7:48

Remember that Moses was told by YHWH in Exodus that he could never see the face of G-D or he would surely die? Yeshua (the only begotten Son of G-D) represented His Father on earth. When this woman of ill repute looked into the face of Yeshua, she was beholding the very face of G-D the Father, and instead of receiving death, she received life, deliverance, healing, and transformation.

How did she receive it? She received it by gazing into the beatific face (*panim*) of Yeshua and hearing His comforting words as she watched them being formed from His lips.

## YHWH PREPARING FOR HIS RETURN

In summary, in the Tanakh (old covenant) G-D kept Moses from seeing His face because of the stain of original sin. In the new covenant Yeshua was the face of the living G-D, made flesh and walking among us (John 1:14). When you looked into Yeshua's eyes, you were looking into the face of G-D!

For in [Yeshua] lives all the fullness of the [Elohim] bodily.

—COLOSSIANS 2:9

Today, we who are believers in Messiah are called to be the face of G-D for others to see! For the most part, believers today can accept that we can approach YHWH (our heavenly Father) through His only begotten Son, Yeshua. But we still don't understand that the main reason Yeshua died on the cross was to make a way for us to access and know YHWH (our heavenly Father) in the most intimate way. Being spiritually face-to-face with Him, being embraced by Him, and then being able to see His visage is something that YHWH is ready to bring about in this age before His return to earth with Yeshua.

> I, John, saw the Holy City, the New Jerusalem, coming down out of heaven from [G-D the heavenly Father], prepared as a bride adorned for her husband [Yeshua]. And I heard a loud voice from heaven, saying, "Look! The tabernacle of [G-D, YHWH] is with men, and He will dwell with them. They shall be His people, and [G-D] Himself [the heavenly Father] will be with them and be their [G-D, Father]. '[G-D] shall wipe away all tears from their eyes. There shall be no more death.' Neither shall there be any more sorrow nor crying nor pain, for the former things have passed away."
>
> —REVELATION 21:2–4

I submit to you that YHWH (our heavenly Father), in preparation for His return with Yeshua His only begotten Son, is making Himself known again through the Priestly Prayer of the Blessing in a more tangible way.

One of today's worship songs, "Show Me Your Face" by Don Potter, shares the desire and yearning of YHWH (our heavenly Father) to show forth His face to us. For more of Don Potter's music, visit www.potterhausmusic.net.

> Moses stood on the mountain waiting for You to pass by
> You put Your hand over his face so in Your presence he
> wouldn't die
> All of Israel saw the glory and it shines down through the age
> Now You've called me to boldly seek Your face
>
> Show me Your face, Lord, show me Your face
> And gird up my legs that I might stand in this holy place
> Show me Your face, Lord, Your power and grace

I could make it to the end if I could just see Your face

David knew there was something more than the ark of Your
   presence
In a manger a baby was born among kings and peasants
All of Israel saw the glory and it shines down through the age
Now You've called us to boldly seek Your face

We will make it to the end if we could just see Your face
I will make it to the end, Abba [Father], show me Your face[2]

In our Bibles we read this portion of the divine prayer:

The LORD make His *face* [to be accessible to you]...
                                              —NUMBERS 6:25

But there's more! YHWH is not only making His face accessible
to you. In the next chapter we will dig deep into what it means for
Him to make His face *shine upon you.*

## KEYS TO THE BLESSING

Under the Old Covenant Moses was told he could not see the
face of YHWH or he would surely die, yet even in the Old Testament scriptures later on we were encouraged to seek His face.
Through this Priestly Prayer of the Blessing, G-D our Father is
making His face available for us to behold.

## STUDY QUESTIONS

What benefits do you receive when you are able to look in the
face of another person, rather than communicate from a distance?

_____

_____

_____

What happened when the woman of ill repute looked into the eyes of Yeshua (Jesus) who represented the very face of G-D the Father?

_____

_____

_____

What did Yeshua accomplish by His death on the cross for us concerning our gaining access to our heavenly Father?

_____

_____

_____

## Chapter 13

# THE HEBREW WORD FOR SHINE

# אוֹר

*Or,* meaning "light divided from the darkness"
(Hebrew is read from right to left)

THE NEXT ABSTRACT word in the Priestly Prayer of the Blessing is *shine.*

> The LORD bless you and keep you; the LORD make His face to *shine* upon you.
>
> —NUMBERS 6:24–25

In the first portion of the Priestly Prayer of the Blessing YHWH (your heavenly Father) kneels in front of you, His spiritual son or daughter, as a good parent desiring to make Himself available and minister to you. In the second portion your heavenly Father places His arms around you with a divine embrace, holding you in His strong arms of protection and security. In the third portion it's as if He loosens His divine embrace and while still keeping His holy hands upon your shoulders, He pulls away enough for you to see Him face-to-face so you can experience His reality and person.

We are now going to explore what it means for YHWH (your heavenly Father) to make His face shine upon you! To get started, we need to understand that in Hebraic thought, light equates to order and darkness to chaos.

> In the beginning [G-D] created the heavens and the earth. The earth was formless and void, darkness [chaos] was over the surface of the deep, and the Spirit of [G-D] was moving over the surface of the water. [G-D] said, "Let there be light [order]," and there was light [order]. [G-D] saw that the light [order] was good, and [G-D] separated the light [order] from the darkness [chaos].
>
> —GENESIS 1:1–4

By amplifying the verses above with this concept, we see that when the earth was without form, void, and in the dark, there was chaos. Light had to be created first so that YHWH could bring order. When the Priestly Prayer of the Blessing is proclaimed over you by Yeshua (Jesus) our High Priest, you will find that the face of G-D shining upon you brings order. As the Father imparts a portion of Himself upon you, your thoughts will become singular.

The enemy of our souls loves to bring confusion. As the enemy attacks us with circumstances, trials, and challenges, we often find ourselves embroiled in conflicting thoughts. We often become apprehensive and disquieted, and sometimes this leads to oppression or even depression. Many times we are conflicted and puzzled when making decisions.

Yet when the face of YHWH (our heavenly Father) begins to shine upon us, we sense that everything is going to be OK. Suddenly we become single-minded. Our thoughts become aligned with His thoughts.

Just as YHWH said at creation, "Let there be light," to bring to order that which was in darkness and chaos, so too this occurs when we can spiritually see His face (*panim*) because His face is the source of illumination—of light. *Or* is the Hebrew word for shine, and it connotes that when the light of His face begins to shine upon you, He brings order into your life. Chaos, wrong thinking, and conflicting thoughts must leave. Your God-given purpose, your calling becomes crystal clear. You suddenly begin to understand the revelation of a step-by-step process that will help you begin to fulfill whatever your God-given assignment on earth truly is.

Confusion is gone, conflicting thoughts are gone, and the enemy's interference is negated. Now, YHWH is ready to begin His creation—His restoration—His breathing new life into you so that you can move to the next level of His glory.

The Hebrew word for restoration is *arukah.* "The biblical meaning is to receive back more than has been lost to the point that the final state is greater than the original condition. Unlike the regular dictionary's meaning of *restoration,* which is to return something back to its original condition, the biblical definition of the word has greater connotations that go above and beyond the typical everyday usage."[1]

When the face of YHWH (our heavenly Father) radiates the glory light of His presence toward you, things are transformed. The children of Israel became slaves in Egypt by a wicked taskmaster, Pharaoh. G-D appeared to Moses in the burning bush in the wilderness. It was the light of His very person in that bush, and Moses heard the voice of G-D projecting out from the light of G-D's face shining onto him.

Moses received clear instructions. He was assigned the task of being G-D's chosen vessel to deliver the children of Israel out of bondage. More than His delivering them out of the hands of Pharaoh, YHWH wanted to impart a covenant relationship with them where He (YHWH) would call them into order. He did this through imparting His *Torah* (His instructions, precepts, and commandments) so they could thrive even in the midst of the desert.

In Exodus 23 G-D promises seven specific blessings to those who walk in His precepts and fellowship with Him during His weekly Sabbath and in His appointed times, the seven feasts of YHWH.

+ He will send an angel before you to guard you.

+ He will be an enemy to your enemies.

+ He will bless you with provision.

+ He will remove sickness from you.

+ There will be no miscarrying or barrenness among you.

+ He will fulfill the number of your days, and you will not die early.

+ You will become fruitful and take possession of the land.

Then again YHWH appeared to Moses on Mount Sinai in the form of the Shekinah glory, His very face beaming and causing Moses's face to shine with the reflection of G-D's glory. In the midst of the glory is where YHWH gave Moses the Ten Commandments written by His own finger. You see, the greatest communication comes when we are close to the face of G-D our Father *shining* upon us!

Moses then spent time with G-D in the temporary dwelling place, the tent of meeting, standing in the Shekinah glory. It was there in the midst of the glory where the one true G-D imparted to Moses His precepts and instruction as contained in the Torah. All this was given to bring order out of the chaos and the darkness that Satan had wrought on the earth, deceiving even the very elite, since the fall of Adam and Eve.

After Moses received the Ten Commandments, YHWH gave Moses the Priestly Prayer of the Blessing. When this portion of the divine prayer is proclaimed over you in the name (*shem*) of Yeshua the Jewish High Priest in heaven, the very face of your heavenly Father will shine upon you as it did to Moses. The face of Moses began to shine from the reflection of being in the presence of the Shekinah glory—the illumination of the very face (*panim*) of G-D shining out from the midst of the cloud toward him.

The impartation of the words of the Torah came to Moses while spending time in the Shekinah glory of the Most High G-D. Enlightenment comes to us, opening up understanding from the Word of G-D, which proceeds out of the face of our heavenly Father illuminating upon us His revelation. When G-D spoke during creation, things came into existence.

> [G-D] said, "Let there be light," and there was light.
> —GENESIS 1:3

> Then [G-D] said, "Let there be an expanse in the midst of the waters, and let it separate the waters from the waters."...And it was so.
> —GENESIS 1:6–7

> Then [G-D] said, "Let the waters under the heavens be gathered together into one place, and let the dry land appear." And it was so.
> —GENESIS 1:9

When YHWH appears before you face-to-face as a result of this portion of the Priestly Prayer of the Blessing, His face shines upon you. His mouth proceeds to declare words of blessing and promises that come alive as they ignite and bear fruit in your life! Darkness is dispelled.

The Hebrew word *or* also speaks of a door or a portal. It is order that opens the door to the next level, to the next opportunity, and into the supernatural of G-D.

When the face of your heavenly Father shines upon you, there is a doorway or portal to heaven opened. When the face of YHWH comes close to you and you gaze into His loving eyes, you begin to see heavenly things.

## Doorways to Heaven in the Old Testament

Doorways or portals into heaven are talked about in the Tanakh (Old Testament). Prior to G-D's covenant with Moses and the children of Israel, these portals were avenues where angels could ascend and descend, and certain individuals were able to get a glimpse of what was in heaven.

Jacob, whose name was changed by G-D to Israel, discovered a heavenly portal. Jacob spent the night in a place where his grandfather Abraham had "called upon the name of the Lord" (Gen. 13). Jacob fell asleep with his head propped up on a "covenant stone." His dream was so real that it transformed his life.

> [Jacob] came to a certain place and stayed there all night, because the sun had set. He took one of the stones of that place and put it under his head, and lay down in that place to sleep. He dreamed and saw a ladder set up on the earth with the top of it reaching to heaven. The angels of [G-D] were ascending and descending on it. [YHWH] stood above it and said, "I am the Lord [G-D] of Abraham your father and the [G-D] of Isaac. The land on which you lie, to you will I give it and to your descendants. Your descendants will be like the dust of the earth, and you will spread abroad to the west and to the east and to the north and to the south, and in you and in your descendants all the families of the earth will be blessed. Remember, I am with you, and I will protect you wherever you go, and I will bring you back to this land. For I will not leave you until I have done what I promised you."
>
> Jacob awoke out of his sleep, and he said, "Surely [YHWH] is in this place, and I did not know it." He was afraid and said, "How awesome is this place! This is none other but the house of [G-D], and this is the gate of heaven."
>
> —Genesis 28:11–17

A portal opened for Jacob, which was a way he could glimpse into heaven and see YHWH in the form of His Shekinah glory. In addition, he received a word that echoed the same promises concerning the land of Israel as an inheritance that YHWH gave to his father, Isaac, and his grandfather Abraham. Jacob made a pillar out of the stone upon which he had laid his head. Jacob called it the "Dwelling Place of YHWH (YeHoVaH or YaHWeH)."

Ezekiel the prophet also experienced the portal or door into heaven even in the midst of the Babylonian captivity of the children of Israel. In fact, he experienced an even greater portal opened up to him.

> In the thirtieth year, in the fourth month, on the fifth day of the month, as I was among the captives by the river of Kebar, the heavens were opened and I saw visions of [YHWH]....
>
> The hand of the LORD was upon me there, and [YHWH] said to me, Rise, go out into the plain, and I will talk with you there. Then I arose, and went out into the plain. And the glory of [YHWH] stood there, as the glory which I saw by the river of Kebar, and I fell on my face.
>
> —EZEKIEL 1:1; 3:22–23

Not only did he see into heaven and behold the Shekinah glory of YHWH (YeHoVaH or YaHWeH), but he experienced the impartation of the power of the glory as it was emitted from the face (*panim*) of G-D shining down upon him.

King David, under the inspiration of the Ruach HaKodesh (Holy Spirit), wrote about the appearance of YHWH in the glory as He comes through such a door or portal.

> Lift up your heads, O you gates [portals]; and be lifted up, you everlasting doors, that the King of glory may enter. Who is this King of glory? [YHWH] strong and mighty, [YHWH] mighty in battle.
>
> —PSALM 24:7–8

## DOORWAYS TO HEAVEN IN THE NEW TESTAMENT

Yeshua said that He was the only way to heaven, whereby we have access to YHWH (the heavenly Father).

> I am the door. If anyone enters through Me, he will be saved and will go in and out and find pasture.
>
> —JOHN 10:9

> [Yeshua] said to him, "I am the way [door], the truth, and the life. No one comes to the Father except through Me."
>
> —JOHN 14:6

Yeshua was alluding to His being like the "Door of the Tabernacle." There was only one way to go into the tabernacle (which was a type or foreshadow of the heavenly tabernacle). Yeshua was saying that He was that door!

Yeshua opened a portal or a door by which we can now have access to the Father. We can by faith go into the holy of holies in heaven (G-D's throne room) where Yeshua is seated at the right hand of the Father, Yeshua's throne being the heavenly mercy seat.

> Let us then come with confidence to the throne of grace, that we may obtain mercy and find grace to help in time of need.
>
> —HEBREWS 4:16

When this portion of the divine prayer is pronounced over you in the name (*shem*) of Yeshua your High Priest, you do not have to go up by faith into the heavenly throne room, but rather it is the face of YHWH (your heavenly Father) coming down from heaven to shine upon you.

Paul shares how the end of our journey is ultimately seeing G-D face-to-face. Our spiritual journey on earth is likened to looking in a mirror and beholding not just our image but the image of YHWH (our heavenly Father) reflecting back at us.

> When I was a child, I spoke as a child, I understood as a child, and I thought as a child. But when I became a man, I put away childish things. For now we see as through a glass, dimly, but then, face to face. Now I know in part, but then I shall know, even as I also am known.
>
> —I CORINTHIANS 13:11–12

Of course, the fullness of seeing G-D our Father face-to-face will occur after the resurrection when our bodies are instantly changed from that which is corruptible to that which is immortal! At that time, we won't just be spiritual sons and daughters of G-D, but we will be physical children of G-D as well. Yet we need to know that in this period of end-time preparation for the return of YHWH (our heavenly Father) and Yeshua, when New Jerusalem descends from heaven onto the earth, that through the "rediscovery" on how to proclaim over ourselves G-D's Priestly Prayer of the Blessing, we can begin to have G-D's face (*panim*) shining His glory upon us now! When this happens, it will usher us into being transformed from one level of glory to the next.

Nevertheless when anyone turns to the Lord, the veil is removed. Now the Lord is the Spirit. And where the Spirit of the Lord is, there is liberty. But we all, seeing the glory of [YHWH] with unveiled faces, as in a mirror, are being transformed into the same image from glory to glory by the Spirit of the Lord.

—2 Corinthians 3:16–18

## The Face of YHWH Is Shining Upon You

When YHWH (our heavenly Father) shines His face (*panim*) upon you, His order is imparted to you and your thoughts become His thoughts.

Finally, brothers, whatever things are true, whatever things are honest, whatever things are just, whatever things are pure, whatever things are lovely, whatever things are of good report, if there is any virtue, and if there is any praise, think on these things.

—Philippians 4:8

When the face of G-D shines upon you, you won't have to strive to place your mind in subjection to meditate on such thoughts. It's not you having to try and take every thought captive to obtain the "Mind of Messiah."

For the weapons of our warfare are not of the flesh but have *divine power* to destroy strongholds. We destroy arguments and every lofty opinion raised against the knowledge of [YHWH], and take every thought captive to obey [Messiah].

—2 Corinthians 10:4–5, esv

By default of being in such intimacy with our heavenly Father, you receive divine thinking that overpowers your own thoughts and human reasoning with His perfect and pure thoughts! An outpouring of His grace transfers to you through the illumination of His glory.

## My Personal Testimony of a Face-to-Face Encounter With YHWH

In the last few years, as the reality of this teaching was revealed to me, I had a powerful encounter with YHWH my heavenly Father.

I was lying on my bed, starting to come out of a good night's sleep yet not quite awake, when suddenly I saw a face close to my face.

The face was shining with a golden hue, and I could see beautiful eyes—full of compassion and love. I saw a mouth that had the most beatific smile. The rest of the features were hard to discern, but I felt a tremendous peace. It was the same peace I felt as a five-year-old child when I had the dream of being in heaven and experienced the Shekinah glory of YHWH.

I realized that I was feeling "indescribable bliss" as a result of the face I was beholding, and I said to myself, "I want to feel like this all the time!" The thought came to me, "I am Abba—your Father." The next thing I knew, I yelled out, "Father!" I sensed the breath from the mouth of His face breathing into my nostrils. I inhaled deeply and experienced an impartation, my soul awakening to a new sense of the Shekinah glory of the one true G-D of Israel.

When I had first recognized Yeshua as my Messiah and my Lord (Adonai), I had a powerful sense of peace and joy that flooded my entire being. Yet this encounter with the face of YHWH (my heavenly Father) was far greater than anything I'd ever experienced before. For over two years every day I had been proclaiming the Priestly Prayer of the Blessing over myself in the name (*shem*) of my High Priest Yeshua. What I noticed was that unlike any time before, my thoughts were not conflicted.

All I could dwell on was the face that appeared before me and the person of my heavenly Father.

My entire being felt centered on the Most High G-D! It wasn't due to any effort on my part. It was the result of the appearance of the very face of the one true G-D. He was bringing order to my life. It was His face shining upon me. The Hebrew word for shine is *or*, and it also means "to ignite, to set on fire, to bring revival."

The moment I shouted out, "Father!" and experienced Him breathing His breath into my nostrils, I sensed an impartation of new life—of inspiration—I felt like I was resurrected from the dead. As a result, my very thoughts became His—my stream of consciousness was single-minded on the things of G-D. I felt like I was in perfect sync with the one true G-D of Israel.

He gave me a list of items that I need to accomplish for the kingdom in the exact order in which I was to complete each task. He then gave me the method to realize these tasks. Some required the engaging of other people. I sensed that He was helping me to take charge of my life by the power of the Holy Spirit to accomplish my God-given destiny, calling, and purpose.

After my encounter with the face of G-D, I opened my Bible and was directed to the following scripture about the relationship between YHWH (our heavenly Father) and Yeshua. Even greater than this, I was able to see for myself what the grand finale of the second coming of Yeshua will usher in.

> Have this mind among yourselves, which is yours in [Messiah Yeshua], who, though he was in the form of [YHWH, the heavenly Father], did not count equality with [G-D] a thing to be grasped, but emptied himself, by taking the form of a servant, being born in the likeness of men. And being found in human form, he humbled himself by becoming obedient to the point of death, even death on a cross. Therefore [YHWH, our heavenly Father] has highly exalted him and bestowed on him the name that is above every name, so that at the name of [Yeshua] every knee should bow, in heaven and on earth and under the earth, and every tongue confess that [Yeshua HaMashiach] is Lord [Adonai], to the glory of [G-D] the Father.
>
> —PHILIPPIANS 2:5–11, ESV

The above scripture shares that YHWH has given Yeshua a name above every name. Yet I have never understood what was revealed to me next as I turned to the next scripture.

> But in fact, [Messiah] has been raised from the dead. [Messiah] is the first of a great harvest of all who have died. So you see, just as death came into the world through a man [Adam], now the resurrection from the dead has begun through another man [Yeshua, Jesus]. Just as everyone dies because we all belong to Adam, everyone who belongs to [Messiah] will be given new life. But there is an order to this resurrection: [Messiah] was raised as the first of the harvest; then all who belong to [Messiah] will be raised when [Messiah] comes back.
>
> —1 CORINTHIANS 15:20–23, NLT

The above scripture is talking about the order of the resurrection being the death and resurrection of Yeshua first, followed by all who are believers and under the new covenant being raised (or raptured) during the return of Yeshua. Those who were dead will be resurrected first, then we who are alive shall also be raptured, and our bodies will be changed from that which is mortal to immortal. We will not just be spiritual sons and daughters of G-D, but physical sons and daughters. We will be like Yeshua Himself.

Yet here is the portion of the passage that really blew me away!

> After that the end will come, when [Yeshua, Jesus] will turn the Kingdom over to [YHWH, G-D the Father], having destroyed every ruler and authority and power. For [Messiah] must reign until [G-D the Father] humbles all [Yeshua's] enemies beneath [Messiah's] feet. And the last enemy to be destroyed is death. For the Scriptures say, "[G-D the Father] has put all things under [Yeshua's] authority." Of course, when it says "all things are under [Yeshua's] authority," that does not include [G-D the Father] himself, who gave [Messiah] his authority. Then, when all things are under [Yeshua's] authority, the Son will put himself under [G-D the Father's] authority, so that [G-D the Father], who gave his Son authority over all things, will be utterly supreme over everything everywhere.
>
> —1 Corinthians 15:24–28, nlt

What stunned me about this passage is it clearly states that though Yeshua's name is above every name, His name is not above the name of the Father. Here in this grand finale we see that "the Son will put himself under [G-D the Father's] authority, so that [G-D the Father], who gave his Son authority over all things, will be utterly supreme over everything everywhere."

The grand finale of all things is when our heavenly Father will be utterly supreme over everything everywhere! I was stunned to find this out. Immediately I heard the still, small voice of G-D say, "So Warren, what are you waiting for?" If the end of all things is that YHWH (our heavenly Father) will be utterly supreme over everything everywhere, shouldn't we be ready for the Father to reveal Himself to us now through His Priestly Prayer of the Blessing? This is why I know I was given the awesome responsibility to share how we can gain ultimate access to YHWH (our heavenly Father) through this divine prayer!

## THE SHINING FACE OF G-D
## IMPARTS REVELATION

It is from the face of G-D that we receive instruction. His mouth whispers words when He is close to us. His Word is a lamp to our feet—it lights the way, the path, the narrow road that we should follow.

> Your word is a lamp to my feet and a light to my path.
>
> —PSALM 119:105

It's not a struggle when we are in His presence. We become centered, not wanting to go to the left or the right without His instruction or beckoning. Sometimes He is directing us to retreat! Other times He gently compels us to stay perfectly still, waiting and basking in Him as He appears to us in the form of the Shekinah glory. We are to wait so we can be replenished, strengthened, invigorated, and bathed in heavenly downloads of His instruction and His revelation.

> But those who wait on the LORD shall renew their strength; they shall mount up with wings as eagles, they shall run and not be weary, and they shall walk and not faint.
>
> —ISAIAH 40:31

Since that day my life has never been the same. As I proclaim the Priestly Prayer of the Blessing over myself, in the manner in which YHWH instructed, in the name (*shem*) of Yeshua my High Priest—I find myself more in sync moment by moment each day with the one true G-D of Israel's plans for my life.

It is normal for me now to be in constant communication with the Father, even when I'm doing minimal tasks, when I'm watching the news on TV, when I'm driving in my car, when people are talking to me. I sense Him helping me to filter the conversation in light of eternity. My level of discernment has been sharpened.

The Book of Hebrews declares that mature religion is having your senses exercised to discern both good and evil.

> But solid food belongs to those who are of full age (*spiritually mature*), that is, those who by reason of use have their *senses exercised* to discern both good and evil.
>
> —HEBREWS 5:14, NKJV

When the face of the Father comes close to you, you begin to see through His eyes and hear through His ears. You begin to be able to smell the atmosphere, whether it is of G-D or of the enemy! Your heart becomes filled with the things of G-D and eternity—you become full of compassion! Your mind is no longer conflicted, having to cast down ungodly imaginations, fleshly temptations, evil, or accusations of the enemy! Instead your mind is filled with those things that are good, lovely, and of good report (Phil. 4:8).

Each day when I proclaim the Priestly Prayer of the Blessing over myself, I find that He and His Ruach HaKodesh become stronger in me. I am enabled to function at a higher level with all the responsibilities I have first as a husband, a father, and a grandfather, and with all of the many tasks I have to perform in my job and ministry.

Many people who work alongside of me on a daily basis ask me, "How are you able to accomplish so much?" I believe that all glory must go to G-D for first revealing the reality of Yeshua as being my Messiah and Lord (Adonai) when I received the new birth, and then placing the Ruach HaKodesh (Holy Spirit) within me and upon me. Yet, greatest of all, is the Father now making Himself known to me in the most tangible way.

For me, it began with YHWH (the heavenly Father) revealing Himself to me in the form of the Shekinah glory in the dream I had as a little boy. I know now that my main purpose for being born is to share the revelation that through this Priestly Prayer of the Blessing you too can enter into a life guided by the power of the Most High G-D. Like never before you will experience the supernatural power to accomplish your divine calling, purpose, and destiny!

It is one thing to be successful, but many times our achievements can be built on the "dead bodies" of others! The most impressive thing I have heard others say to me is that they have observed my attitude as being "full of peace, gentleness, and humility." When conflicts arise and the pressures from deadlines come, even in the midst of the enemy's attacks, I have been able to exhibit the "fruit of the Ruach HaKodesh." This is not to my credit at all, but instead, it is because I have now been given the key to having access to the Father Himself, along with intimacy with Yeshua and the Ruach HaKodesh.

When the face of YHWH is close to you, His voice is released in whispers—the still, small voice of the Lord G-D Almighty is constantly communicating to His spiritual sons and daughters.

In our English Bibles we read this portion stated as:

The LORD make His face to shine upon you.

—NUMBERS 6:25

But in the amplified Hebrew-to-English translation it is:

May YHWH (YeHoVaH, YaHWeH, your heavenly Father) illuminate the *wholeness* of His *being* toward you, continually bringing *order*, so that you will fulfill your God-given destiny and purpose.

## KEYS TO THE BLESSING

In creation when G-D said, "Let there be light," it brought order out of the chaos and darkness that existed so that He could begin creation. So too when His face illuminates light upon you, it is so He can bring restoration and bring you to the next level of His glory!

## STUDY QUESTIONS

When you are face-to-face with the Father, what do you want to share with Him? What do you want to ask Him for?

_____

_____

_____

What does it mean when G-D opens heavenly portals or doors to you?

_____

_____

_____

When G-D's face shines upon you, what attributes does this
bring into your life?

_____

_____

_____

# Chapter 14

# THE HEBREW WORD FOR GRACIOUS

## חנן

Chanan, meaning "to show favor to"
(Hebrew is read from right to left)

THE NEXT WORD in the Priestly Prayer of the Blessing is *gracious*.

The LORD make His face to shine upon you, and be *gracious*
unto you.

—NUMBERS 6:25

What does it mean for G-D to be gracious to you when the face of YHWH (your heavenly Father) is shining upon you? The Hebrew word for gracious is *chanan*, which means "to show unmerited favor." Other meanings are "to exhibit a yearning toward, demonstrate a longing for, be merciful to, exhibit compassion, be inclined toward, be considerate of, and demonstrate a desire to spare." When we see how the Hebrew word for gracious is used in Scripture, we can better appreciate what our heavenly Father will demonstrate to us when we see Him face-to-face.

**I will hear because I am gracious.**

If you lend money to any of My people who is poor among you, do not be a creditor to him, and do not charge him interest. If you take your neighbor's garment as a pledge, you shall return it to him before the sun goes down, for that is his only covering; it is his garment for his body. In what else will he sleep? And when he cries out to Me, I will hear, for *I am gracious*.

—EXODUS 22:25–27

179

**I am longsuffering.**

> Then the LORD descended in the cloud, and stood with him there, and proclaimed the name of the LORD. The LORD passed by before him, and proclaimed, *"The LORD, the LORD [G-D], merciful and gracious, slow to anger, and abounding in goodness and truth, keeping mercy for thousands, forgiving iniquity and transgression and sin, but who will by no means clear the guilty, visiting the iniquity of fathers on the children and on the children's children, to the third and the fourth generation."*
>
> —EXODUS 34:5–7

**I am compassionate and merciful.**

> Because if you return to the LORD, your brothers and children will find compassion before those who have taken them captive, in order to return you to this land. *For the LORD your [G-D] is gracious and compassionate.* He will not turn His face from you if you all return to Him.
>
> —2 CHRONICLES 30:9

**I am slow to anger.**

> But You, O Lord, are a [G-D] full of compassion and gracious, *slow to anger,* and abundant in mercy and truth.
>
> —PSALM 86:15, NKJV

## AN EXAMPLE OF THE GRACIOUSNESS OF YHWH

The children of Israel in the wilderness had witnessed the Egyptians humbled by ten horrible plagues. Yet YHWH didn't harm any of them.

- ✦ They were delivered from the slavery of an evil taskmaster—the Pharaoh of Egypt. The hand of YHWH rescued them.

- ✦ They beheld YHWH's pillar of fire keeping the mighty army of Egypt at bay.

- ✦ They marveled at the power of YHWH as the Red Sea was parted.

- ♦ They watched as the Egyptian army was destroyed before their eyes as the waters fell upon them.

- ♦ They beheld the cloud of the Shekinah glory and the thundering of YHWH's voice from Mount Sinai.

Even though they had witnessed the mighty power and benevolence of their G-D, they became frightened, not knowing if Moses was coming back since he had been gone for forty days and nights. While Moses was away on Mount Sinai meeting with G-D, the children of Israel convinced Aaron, who would become the high priest, to build them a golden calf to worship in place of the one true G-D of Israel.

> Now when the people saw that Moses delayed coming down from the mountain, the people gathered themselves together around Aaron and said to him, "Come, make us gods which will go before us. As for this Moses, the man who brought us up out of the land of Egypt, we do not know what has become of him."
>
> —Exodus 32:1

Moses was receiving the Ten Commandments written by YHWH's own finger. The first commandment reads:

> You shall have no other gods before Me. You shall not make for yourself any graven idol, any likeness *of anything* that *is* in heaven above, or that *is* in the earth beneath, or that is in the water below the earth.
>
> —Exodus 20:3–4

Aaron took from the children of Israel the spoils of Egypt and fashioned them into a false god, a golden calf. Aaron had used the gold and silver, which was earmarked to build the tabernacle in the wilderness where the one true G-D would come and dwell inside the holy of holies in the form of the Shekinah glory.

> So they rose up early on the next day, and offered burnt offerings, and brought peace offerings. And the people sat down to eat and to drink, and rose up to play.
>
> —Exodus 32:6

[YHWH] spoke to Moses, "Go, and get down, for your people, whom you brought out of the land of Egypt, have corrupted themselves....Now therefore let Me alone, so that My wrath may burn against them and I may destroy them. And I will make of you a great nation."

—Exodus 32:7, 10

But Moses reminded YHWH that the children of Israel were G-D's chosen people and that He had made promises to Abraham, Isaac, and Jacob that were everlasting covenants whereby their seed would inherit the land forever. Moses pleaded with G-D and said that it would look bad if He delivered them from the hand of Pharaoh only to consume them in the wilderness—and G-D heard Moses!

[YHWH] relented of the harm which He said He would to do to His people.

—Exodus 32:14

This was true grace. Even when they were disobedient, G-D continued to bless them. YHWH created the Priestly Prayer of the Blessing for the children of Israel so that He might place His name (*shem*) upon them. This same prayer is available to us today, which allows us to walk in G-D's very person, His holy character, and His power and authority.

## THE GRACIOUSNESS OF YHWH TODAY

As believers, we can understand these are the qualities Yeshua (Jesus) demonstrated time and time again. Yet we aren't as quick to realize that Yeshua was demonstrating the Father heart of YHWH.

This portion of the Priestly Prayer of the Blessing is about G-D imparting these things to us through the illumination of His very face as He looks into our eyes and we look back into His. Through the new birth He has become our Father—our Daddy—but we don't comprehend with our natural minds how much He loves us. There is no greater and purer love we can ever experience.

When Yeshua was beginning His ministry, He was fully immersed in the *mikvah* (baptism) by John the Baptist. Yeshua went fully under the water of the Jordan River. When He emerged, the Shekinah glory of YHWH began to shine upon Him. It was the glory of the face of YHWH smiling and beaming His love and acceptance.

And when [Yeshua] was baptized [fully immersed], He came up immediately out of the water. And suddenly the heavens were opened to Him [a door opened], and He saw the [Ruach HaKodesh] descending on Him like a dove. And a voice came from heaven, saying, "This is My beloved Son, in whom I am well pleased."

—MATTHEW 3:16–17

This was YHWH (the heavenly Father) giving His graciousness—in Hebrew, His *chanan*. It's not just what was said to Yeshua. The truth is Yeshua could sense the love and approval of His Father.

Through the new birth, He is our heavenly Father. When YHWH (our heavenly Father) shines His face (*panim*) upon us, He is not only imparting order, destiny, and purpose, but He is also showing forth His love and approval. If you and I could see His loving, compassionate eyes as this portion of the divine prayer is proclaimed over us, we would melt and weep uncontrollably. There is no greater love that we could ever experience.

YHWH (your heavenly Father) is saying to you the same thing He did to Yeshua, His only begotten Son, "You are My beloved son or daughter, in whom I am well pleased." YHWH is looking past your shortcomings, your failures, and your weaknesses, and through G-D's greatest prayer of grace—the only prayer in the entire Bible written by Him—He is making available His face to shine upon you so that you will know His love in the greatest way possible. He is bringing His reassurance to you, "You are My beloved spiritual son or daughter. I love you."

## THE AMPLIFIED HEBREW-TO-ENGLISH MEANING

Other root words derived from the Hebrew word *chanan* mean that G-D will be gracious, providing love, sustenance, and friendship. It is favor far beyond what we deserve. In our English Bibles we read:

The LORD make His face to shine upon you, and be *gracious unto you.*

—NUMBERS 6:25

With the Hebrew meaning in mind, the amplified Hebrew-to-English translation is this:

May YHWH [YeHoVaH, YaHWeH, your heavenly Father] provide you with perfect love and fellowship [never leaving you] and give you sustenance [provision] and friendship.

## SEE IT IN YOUR MIND'S EYE

YHWH *blesses* you…

In the first portion of the Priestly Prayer of the Blessing YHWH kneels in front of you, His spiritual son or daughter, as a good parent desiring to make Himself available and minister to you.

YHWH *keeps* you…

In this second portion YHWH places His arms around you with a divine embrace, holding you in His strong arms of protection and security.

YHWH makes His *face* to come into view before you…

In this portion of the Priestly Prayer of the Blessing it's as if He loosens His divine embrace and while still keeping His holy hands upon your shoulders, He pulls away enough for you to see Him face-to-face so you can begin experience His reality and person.

Then YHWH makes His to face *shine* upon you!

In this portion of the Priestly Prayer of the Blessing YHWH (your heavenly Father) reveals His perfect love to you as your Daddy with loving eyes and a beatific smile. He looks past your weaknesses and your frailties, pledging that He will never leave you and that He will provide you with His love and fellowship and friendship.

It is your heavenly Father saying to you, "You are My beloved son or daughter, in whom I am well pleased." It is an impartation where you will know that you are never alone and He is for you and not against you. The Bible puts it this way:

> For I am persuaded that neither death nor life, neither angels
> nor principalities nor powers, neither things present nor things
> to come, neither height nor depth, nor any other created thing,

shall be able to separate us from the love of [YHWH], which is in [Messiah Yeshua] our Lord [Adonai].

—ROMANS 8:38–39

## KEYS TO THE BLESSING

Because you are His son or daughter, your heavenly Father looks past your faults and weaknesses and expresses His love and pleasure over you!

## STUDY QUESTIONS

What does it mean for you that YHWH is *your* heavenly Father? What did He say to Yeshua during Yeshua's baptism (*mikvah*) that He also wants to say to you?

_____

_____

_____

What does it mean that your heavenly Father is gracious to you?

_____

_____

_____

## Chapter 15

# THE HEBREW WORD FOR LIFT

# נָשָׂא

*Nasa,* meaning "to lift up continually"
(Hebrew is read from right to left)

Τ HE NEXT WORD in the Priestly Prayer of the Blessing is *lift.*

The LORD *lift* His countenance upon you...

—NUMBERS 6:26

The Hebrew word *nasa,* which is translated in our English Bibles as the word *lift,* literally means "to lift, carry, or take." When this portion of the Priestly Prayer of the Blessing is pronounced over you in the name of Yeshua, our High Priest, your heavenly Father begins to lift you in His strong arms and carry you. When you are lifted up, nothing can harm you, but more importantly YHWH is imparting Himself to you, transferring everything He is and has for you as your loving Daddy.

## SCRIPTURAL REFERENCES TO YHWH LIFTING THOSE HE LOVES

There are many scriptures in the Tanakh (Old Testament) that convey the concept of YHWH (our heavenly Father) lifting us up and carrying us.

He delivers me from my enemies. You [YHWH] lift me up above those who rise up against me; You have delivered me from the violent man.

—PSALM 18:48

The above scripture says YHWH lifted Israel through their journeys and through the proclamation of the Priestly Prayer of the Blessing. You can apply this same scripture to your own life. He will lift *you* up in His strong loving arms to deliver *you* from your enemies, and He will give *you* divine protection from those who rise up against you! This alludes to those who may be close to you, in your own family, or your brethren, but who rise up against you to do you harm.

Here is another great scripture that talks about our heavenly Father lifting us up.

> For in the time of trouble [YHWH] will hide me in His pavilion; in the shelter of His tabernacle He will hide me; He will set me up on a rock. Now my head will be lifted up above my enemies encircling me; therefore I will offer sacrifices of joy in His tabernacle; I will sing, yes, I will sing praises to the LORD.
>
> —PSALM 27:5–6

The above scripture conveys how YHWH (your heavenly Father) through the proclamation of the Priestly Prayer of the Blessing will lift us up in His strong arms:

+ He will protect us in our times of trouble and hide us in His pavilion (His dwelling place).

+ He will transport us into the shelter of the Most High (the "secret place," the heavenly holy of holies), hidden, and set high upon a rock (Yeshua), lifted above every enemy, including Satan and his minions.

Having your head lifted up above your enemies means that all who desire to harm you shall know that you are favored by the one true G-D, YHWH. This is further signified in the scripture from the *Brit Hadashah* (New Testament).

> And He raised us up and seated us together in the heavenly places in [Messiah Yeshua], so that in the coming ages [YHWH] might show the surpassing riches of His grace in kindness toward us in [Messiah Yeshua].
>
> —EPHESIANS 2:6–7

Your response is to humble yourself and offer yourself to your heavenly Daddy as He carries you. You respond with joy and sing praises to His name (His very person). Even when you face the most hopeless situation, G-D will lift you up:

> Be gracious to me, O LORD; consider my trouble from those who
> hate me, O You who lifts me up from the gates of death.
>
> —PSALM 9:13

The above reveals that even when you face death itself, He will be
the One who lifts you up and delivers you. He truly views you as His
son or daughter.

> Then I said to you, "Do not be terrified, or afraid of them. [YHWH]
> who goes before you, He shall fight for you, just as all that He did
> for you in Egypt before your eyes, and in the wilderness, where you
> saw how the LORD your [G-D] carried you, as a man carries his son,
> in all the way that you went, until you came to this place."
>
> —DEUTERONOMY 1:29–31

You should not be terrified or fear those who are against you
and against G-D. Even Israel who was disobedient was protected
by YHWH when they were in the wilderness. The most powerful
statement is that G-D carries you "as a man carries his son." His carrying you is a statement that you are His eternal inheritance (Eph.
2:6–7). It's comforting to know how your heavenly Father views you,
no matter how young or old you are.

> Listen to Me [YHWH], O house of Jacob, and all the remnant of
> the house of Israel, who are borne *by Me* from birth and are car-
> ried from the womb: and even to your old age I am He, and even
> to your graying years I will carry you; I have done it, and I will
> bear you; even I will carry, and will deliver you.
>
> —ISAIAH 46:3–4

G-D views you as a child even when you become old and gray.
He still carries you in His divine arms without fail. Your heavenly
Father carried you when you were in your mother's womb and knew
who you would be before the foundation of the world.

> Blessed be the [G-D] and Father of our Lord [Adonai] Jesus
> Christ [Yeshua the Messiah], who has blessed us with every
> spiritual blessing in the heavenly places in [Messiah], just as He
> [YHWH] chose us in Him before the foundation of the world,
> to be holy and blameless before Him in love; He predestined us
> to adoption as sons to Himself through Jesus Christ [Yeshua

the Messiah] according to the good pleasure of His will, to the praise of the glory of His grace which He [YHWH] graciously bestowed on us in the Beloved.

—EPHESIANS 1:3–6

What does your heavenly Father do as He holds you up in His arms and walks with you? The picture is likened to what a good father would do when carrying his newborn son or daughter in his arms.

[YHWH] your [G-D] in your midst, the Mighty One, will save; He will rejoice over you with gladness, He will quiet you with His love, He will rejoice over you with singing.

—ZEPHANIAH 3:17, NKJV

Can you envision yourself as a little baby as your heavenly Father walks with you, carrying you in His arms, singing over you, perhaps dancing?

+ He saves you by lifting you up and carrying you in His arms.

+ He openly rejoices over you with gladness. Imagine His saying over you wonderful and uplifting words, renewing you with His words of love.

+ He will quiet you with His words of love. This alludes to a father comforting his child who is crying. Your heavenly Father wants to comfort you in times of distress, kissing you on the forehead and your cheeks, emoting His love and empathy toward you.

+ He will rejoice over you with singing. This is a beautiful image of the Father's intimacy with you.

I remember when my two children, Tara and Joseph, were babies. I carried them in my arms on a pillow. They would look up at me as I talked quietly to them words expressing my deep love. I would sing Scripture songs over them. Both of them would begin to smile and try and make sounds. They could sense the love I had for them. When I carried them, and we gazed deep into each other's faces, there was no one in the world except my child and me. They had all my attention.

This is what your heavenly Father desires to do with you as a result of this portion of the divine prayer. In our Bibles we read concerning this portion:

> The LORD lift His countenance upon you…
>
> —NUMBERS 6:26

We've discussed what is meant by the word *lift* in this portion of the divine prayer. In the next chapter I will expound upon the rest of this portion of the Priestly Prayer of the Blessing—what it means concerning His countenance being upon us.

## KEYS TO THE BLESSING

The most intimate expression of your heavenly Father's love for you is when He lifts you up in His arms and carries you. You receive His full attention and His outpouring of love in the most intimate way.

## STUDY QUESTIONS

Are you ready to submit to the love of YHWH as expressed when He lifts you up and carries you? Are you ready to receive His full attention and His outpouring of love in the most intimate way?

_____

_____

_____

I discussed many scriptures in this chapter concerning what it means for YHWH to lift you up and carry you. Which ones do you relate to the most?

_____

_____

_____

# Chapter 16

# THE HEBREW WORD FOR COUNTENANCE

## פ נ י ם

*Panim*, plural form, "entire being"
(Hebrew is read from right to left)

THE NEXT WORD in the Priestly Prayer of the Blessing is *countenance*.

The LORD lift His *countenance* upon you...

—NUMBERS 6:26

The Hebrew word for countenance is again *panim*, which we have already discussed in the chapter about the word *face*. This word is plural because it describes the entire behavioral actions of a person. It means "everything that makes up who you are."

King David wrote of the power of having the "countenance of G-D upon us."

There are many who say, "Who will show us any good?" [YHWH],
lift up the light of Your countenance upon us.

—PSALM 4:6, NKJV

Your heavenly Father has lifted us up in His divine, strong, and loving arms and He carries us. Yet now, like the loving Father He is, we look up at His face as He smiles upon us and hugs us and even lovingly kisses us on our forehead.

## SEE IT IN YOUR MIND'S EYE

YHWH blesses you...

In the first portion of the Priestly Prayer of the Blessing, your heavenly Father kneels in front of you, His spiritual son or daughter, as a good parent desiring to make Himself available and minister to you.

YHWH keeps you...

In this second portion your heavenly Father places His arms around you with a divine embrace, holding you in His strong arms of protection and security.

YHWH makes His face to shine upon you...

In this portion of the Priestly Prayer of the Blessing it's as if He loosens His divine embrace and while still keeping His holy hands upon your shoulders, He pulls away enough for you to see Him face-to-face. You begin to experience His reality and His very person. Your heavenly Father makes His to face shine upon you! This is G-D the Father saying to you, "You are my beloved son or daughter, in whom I am well pleased."

YHWH lifts His countenance upon you...

+ This is your heavenly Father lifting you up with His divine strong arms and carrying you, continually looking down at you as He walks. He is your loving heavenly Father.

+ He is also lifting up *all of who He is* toward you. He is putting all of Himself at your disposal. He is bringing everything that He is to your aid.

+ He is supporting you with *His entire being.* Nothing is being withheld. You have the one true G-D of the universe on your side!

+ He is lifting His gaze continually toward you. Even when you aren't thinking about Him, He is near to you and is watching over you.

+ Your heavenly Father is giving you His full attention moment by moment, each and every day.

## YHWH DESIRES TO MAKE HIMSELF AVAILABLE TO YOU

The Scriptures speak of your heavenly Father desiring to make Himself fully available to you.

> [YHWH] has made from one blood [Adam] every nation of men to live on the entire face of the earth, having appointed fixed times and the boundaries of their habitation, that they should seek [YHWH] so perhaps they might reach for Him and find Him, though He is not far from each one of us. "For in Him we live and move and have our being." As some of your own poets have said, "We are His offspring."
>
> —ACTS 17:26–28

Through Messiah Yeshua, both Jews and Gentiles have been given access to YHWH.

> And [Yeshua, Jesus] came and preached peace to you who were far away and peace to those who were near. For through [Yeshua, Jesus] we both have access by one Spirit to [YHWH].
>
> —EPHESIANS 2:17–18

Through Yeshua we have been "born again" as a spiritual son or daughter of the Most High G-D.

> And because you are sons, [YHWH] has sent forth into our hearts the Spirit of His Son [Yeshua, Jesus], crying, "Abba, Father!" Therefore you are no longer a servant, but a son, and if a son, then an heir of [YHWH] through [the Messiah].
>
> —GALATIANS 4:6–7

Even if you are an orphan, YHWH desires to take care of you as your heavenly Father.

> If my father and my mother forsake me, then the LORD will take me in.
>
> —PSALM 27:10

## The Scriptures Are Clear That
## Your Heavenly Father:

• loves you like no other can love you!

The LORD has appeared to him from afar, saying: "Indeed, I have loved you with an everlasting love; therefore with lovingkindness I have drawn you."

—JEREMIAH 31:3

Consider how much love the Father has given to us, that we should be called children of [G-D]. Therefore the world does not know us, because it did not know Him.

—1 JOHN 3:1

• has compassion on you as a good Father!

Like a father shows compassion to his children, so the LORD gives compassion to those who fear Him.

—PSALM 103:13

Blessed be [G-D], the Father of our Lord [Adonai] Jesus Christ [Yeshua the Messiah], the Father of mercies, and the [G-D] of all comfort.

—2 CORINTHIANS 1:3

• cares for you even when you may be forsaken by others!

Humble yourselves under the mighty hand of [G-D], that He may exalt you in due time. Cast all your care upon Him, because He cares for you.

—1 PETER 5:6–7

• delights in you and takes pleasure in His relationship with you!

For the LORD takes pleasure in His people; He will beautify the meek with salvation.

—PSALM 149:4

The LORD your [G-D] is in your midst, a Mighty One, who will save. He will rejoice over you with gladness, He will renew you with His love, He will rejoice over you with singing.

—ZEPHANIAH 3:17

• desires intimacy with you and to call you by name!

But now, thus says the LORD who created you, O Jacob, and He who formed you, O Israel: Do not fear, for I have redeemed you; I have called you by your name; you are Mine. When you pass through waters, I will be with you. And through the rivers, they shall not overflow you. When you walk through the fire, you shall not be burned, nor shall the flame kindle on you.

—ISAIAH 43:1–2

• gives you continual consideration!

The eyes of the LORD are on the righteous, and His ears are open to their cry.

—PSALM 34:15

• calls you His beloved friend!

The Scripture was fulfilled which says, "Abraham believed [G-D], and it was reckoned to him as righteousness," and he was called the friend of [G-D].

—JAMES 2:23

• raises you even when you are forsaken by your flesh and blood parents and brethren!

If my father and my mother forsake me, then the LORD will take me in.

—PSALM 27:10

• desires to be patient and gentle with You!

The LORD is merciful and gracious, slow to anger, and abounding in mercy.

—PSALM 103:8

The Lord is not slow concerning His promise, as some count slowness. But He is patient with us, because He does not want any to perish, but all to come to repentance.

—2 PETER 3:9

• desires to teach and guide you throughout your life!

I will instruct you and teach you in the way you should go; I will counsel you with my eye on you.

—PSALM 32:8

Thus says the LORD, your Redeemer, the Holy One of Israel: "I am the LORD your [G-D], who teaches you to profit, who leads you in the way you should go."

—ISAIAH 48:17

• encourages and upholds you!

Do not fear, for I am with you; do not be dismayed, for I am your [G-D]. I will strengthen you, I will help you, yes, I will uphold you with My righteous right hand.

—ISAIAH 41:10

• provides for you in ways you may never truly recognize!

The LORD is my shepherd; I shall not want.

—PSALM 23:1

Oh, fear the LORD, you His saints; for the ones who fear Him will not be in need.

—PSALM 34:9

• enjoys bestowing upon you good gifts!

Every good gift and every perfect gift is from above and comes down from the Father of lights, with whom is no change or shadow of turning.

—JAMES 1:17

• is kindhearted and forgiving toward you!

For You, LORD, are good, and forgiving, abounding in kindness to all who call on You.

—PSALM 86:5

Who is a [G-D] like You, bearing iniquity and passing over transgression for the remnant of His inheritance? He does not remain angry forever, because He delights in benevolence. He will again have compassion upon us. He will tread down our iniquities, and cast all of our sins into the depths of the sea.

—MICAH 7:18–19

• disciplines you as a good Father who loves you and desires that you walk in His blessings and promises!

> My son, do not despise the chastening of the LORD, nor be weary of His correction; for whom the LORD loves He corrects, even as a father the son in whom he delights.
> —PROVERBS 3:11–12

## YHWH IS A PERFECT FATHER SUPPLYING YOUR BASIC HUMAN NEEDS

### Perfect love

*Through words*—Just as our natural parents can express their love to their children through the words of kindness, praise, and appreciation, so too YHWH has given us His Word made alive in us as He speaks it over us.

*Through affection*—YHWH also created us with a need to receive physical affection. Through this Priestly Prayer of the Blessing He makes Himself available to us to experientially sense His divine love and embrace!

*Through meaningful time spent together*—In the natural the father or mother who takes time to listen to, play with, or just be with their children communicates that their children are important, worth their time and attention. YHWH makes Himself available to us through His divine prayer as He carries us in His arms and imparts the fullness of Himself, His love, and His pleasure concerning us!

### Security

Every child needs to know the world into which they were born is a safe place to live! They need to know that their parents are there to protect them from harm! YHWH provides the utmost in security to us, His children!

### Significance and purpose

Every person needs to know that their life has a purpose and value. YHWH not only unveils to us His calling, His purpose, and His destiny for our lives while here on earth, but He also enables us to accomplish it.[1]

The promise of YHWH to us is...

I will be a Father to you, and you shall be My sons and daughters, says the Lord Almighty.

—2 Corinthians 6:18

In our English Bibles, this portion of the Priestly Prayer of the Blessing is:

The Lord lift up His *countenance* upon you...

—Numbers 6:26

The amplified Hebrew-to-English translation of this portion is:

May YHWH (YeHoVaH, YaHWeH, your heavenly Father) lift up and carry His fullness of being toward you (bringing everything that He has to your aid), supporting you with His divine embrace and His entire being.

## KEYS TO THE BLESSING

Your heavenly Father is ready to lift you up and carry the wholeness of His being toward you continually through the proclamation of this divine prayer over you!

## STUDY QUESTIONS

What does it mean when the heavenly Father lifts His countenance upon you?

_____

_____

_____

Have you ever experienced such intimacy with your heavenly Father?

_____

_____

_____

# Chapter 17

# THE HEBREW WORD FOR GIVE

## שׂוּם

*Siym*, meaning "to cause it to be established"
(Hebrew is read left to right)

ALL OF THE portions of the Priestly Prayer of the Blessing thus far have dealt with YHWH (your heavenly Father) making Himself available to us so He can impart the greatest gift we could ever receive—having His name (*shem*) placed upon us. I am referring to His very person, His holy character, and His power and authority being imparted to us. This final portion of the divine prayer of the blessing deals with what He desires to give us as a result of His appearance and divine embrace.

The next to the last word in the Priestly Prayer of the Blessing is *give*.

> The LORD lift up His countenance upon you, and *give* you peace.
> —NUMBERS 6:26

The Hebrew word for give is *siym*, which has other meanings: "to put, place, set, appoint, make...lay, put or lay upon, lay (violent) hands on...direct toward, to extend (compassion)...ordain, establish, found, appoint, constitute, make, determine, fix...station...plant...transform into...fashion, work, bring to pass... make for a sign."[1]

As we embark on this chapter about the word *give*, let's begin by contemplating the many things that YHWH our heavenly Father gives us.

## 1. His breath of life

> The Spirit of [G-D] has made me, and the breath of the Almighty has given me life.
> —JOB 33:4

199

YHWH (your heavenly Father) is constantly breathing, inhaling, and exhaling, as we also do.

According to an article in the *Daily Mail* by Claire Bates, scientists have discovered that a couple's breathing patterns and heart rates would sync after sitting close to each other. "They didn't even have to hold hands or talk for this to happen."[2]

As we get closer to our heavenly Father, our breathing will become affected by His. When He exhales, we inhale to receive more of His very breath spiritually so we can be filled with more of His person, His holy character, and His power and authority.

Three days after Yeshua died on the cross on the day of Passover, on the Feast of Firstfruits, Yeshua (Jesus) appeared as the resurrected One before His disciples. He then imparted the nature of G-D through the Holy Spirit to them by breathing upon them.

> So [Yeshua] said to them again, "Peace be with you. As My Father has sent Me, even so I send you." When He had said this, He breathed on them and said to them, "Receive the Holy Spirit."
>
> —JOHN 20:21–22

## 2. Wealth and prosperity

> But you must remember the LORD your [G-D], for it is He who gives you the ability to get wealth, so that He may establish His covenant which He swore to your fathers, as it is today.
>
> —DEUTERONOMY 8:18

Yeshua clarified that it was the Father's heart for us to walk in abundance!

> The thief does not come, except to steal and kill and destroy. I came that they may have life, and that they may have it more abundantly.
>
> —JOHN 10:10

YHWH (our heavenly Father) gives us all we need to accomplish our God-given destiny and purpose!

> Command those who are rich in this world that they not be conceited, nor trust in uncertain riches, but in the living [G-D], who richly gives us all things to enjoy.
>
> —1 TIMOTHY 6:17

### 3. Rest and safety from your enemies

> He gives you rest from all your enemies round about, so that you dwell in safety.
>
> —DEUTERONOMY 12:10

Yeshua tells us that we shouldn't strive, but rather, enter into His light and easy yoke.

> Take My yoke upon you, and learn from Me. For I am meek and lowly in heart, and you will find rest for your souls. For My yoke is easy, and My burden is light.
>
> —MATTHEW 11:29–30

### 4. Strength and power

> O [G-D], You are awesome from Your sanctuaries; the [G-D] of Israel is He who gives strength and power to people. Blessed be [G-D]!
>
> —PSALM 68:35

### 5. Rain for harvest

> They do not say in their heart, "Let us now fear the LORD our [G-D], who gives rain, both the former and the latter, in its season. He reserves for us the appointed weeks of the harvest."
>
> —JEREMIAH 5:24

### 6. Wisdom, knowledge, and joy

> For to a man who is pleasing before Him, [G-D] gives wisdom, knowledge, and joy; but to the sinner He gives the work of gathering and collecting to give him who is pleasing before [G-D]. Also this is vanity and chasing the wind.
>
> —ECCLESIASTES 2:26

### 7. Unmerited favor

> But He gives more grace. For this reason it says: "[G-D] resists the proud, but gives grace to the humble."
>
> —JAMES 4:6

But the greatest thing that your heavenly Father wants to give us is His peace. The Hebrew word is *shalom*, which means so much more than it does in English. Before I can give you the amplified Hebrew-to-English translation of this final portion, we must dig deeper into the Hebrew meaning of the Hebrew word for peace in the next chapter.

## KEYS TO THE BLESSING

All of the portions of the Priestly Prayer of the Blessing prior to this final one which says, "And give you peace," were dealing with your heavenly Father making Himself available to you in a supernatural, experiential, and intimate way through His name (*shem*) being placed upon you. As a result of Him placing His very person, His holy character, His power, and His authority upon you, by default He is ready to impart to you His peace.

## STUDY QUESTIONS

What are some of the meanings for the Hebrew word for give?

_____

_____

_____

What are some of the things that your heavenly Father gives you?

_____

_____

_____

# Chapter 18

# THE HEBREW WORD FOR PEACE

# שָׁלוֹם

*Shalom*, meaning "completeness, wholeness"
(Hebrew is read from right to left)

THE FINAL ABSTRACT word in the Priestly Prayer of the Blessing
is *peace*.

> The LORD bless you and keep you; the LORD make His face to
> shine upon you, and be gracious unto you; the LORD lift His
> countenance upon you, and give you *peace*.
>
> —NUMBERS 6:24–26

This final word in G-D's divine prayer of the blessing is abstract
in both English and Greek. We tend to think of the word *peace* as
meaning "the absence of strife and war," but it is so much more! The
root word is *shalam*, which means "to make amends." This is empha-
sized in Scripture:

> The owner of the pit must make restitution. He must give money
> to their owner, and the dead animal will be his.
>
> —EXODUS 21:34

One of the meanings of *shalom* is "to make restitution." Its main
meaning is also "to restore something and make it even better than
its former or original state."

When we have *shalom*, promises and blessings that were robbed
from us by the enemy of our souls are restored when our heavenly
Father imparts His restorative powers to us. He restores us to a right
relationship with Him through the gift of forgiveness and justifica-
tion. He is able to restore our earthly relationships. And He can even
restore days and years that have been lost to the effects of sin. (See
Joel 2:25.) That has to be greatest evidence of the extravagant nature

of G-D's mercy. Not only can He renew your life and redeem your future, but YHWH can also redeem your past.

The heavenly Father restores sight to the blind, the ability to walk to the crippled, hearing to the deaf, and new, clean skin to the diseased. (See Mark 8:22–26; Matthew 9:2–8; Mark 7:31–37; Luke 5:12–25.) G-D doesn't just heal a condition; He restores life, security, and hope to the brokenhearted!

*Shalom* also includes the idea of "vigor and vitality" in all dimensions of life. In short, *shalom* speaks of holistic ("holy") health for our souls and spirits.

## G-D MAKES ALL THINGS NEW

When the Priestly Prayer of the Blessing is pronounced over us, *shalom* causes us to be able to make up for lost time, bestows new identities, and creates new life! YHWH (our heavenly Father) promises good plans for His people, plans that include a hopeful future!

> For I know the plans that I have for you, says [YHWH], plans for peace and not for evil, to give you a future and a hope.
> —JEREMIAH 29:11

The ultimate peace (*shalom*) will be when YHWH ushers in His kingdom of heaven onto the earth.

> And [G-D] will wipe away every tear from their eyes; there shall be no more death, nor sorrow, nor crying. There shall be no more pain, for the former things have passed away.
> —REVELATION 21:4, NKJV

There will be no sickness, pain, sorrow, or crying, because the joy of the Lord will fill the earth as the perfect peace of YHWH (the heavenly Father) will abide on Planet Earth.

## OUR DAILY HOPE

Yeshua was teaching us how to pray for *shalom* (perfect peace as it is in heaven). The prayer is often referred to as the Lord's Prayer.

> Therefore pray in this manner: Our Father who is in heaven, hallowed be Your name.
> —MATTHEW 6:9

Yeshua is referring to the sacred name of the G-D of Israel, YHWH (YeHoVaH, YaHWeH).

> Your kingdom come; Your will be done on earth, as it is in heaven.
> —MATTHEW 6:10

In heaven there is perfect *shalom*. Through the divine prayer of the Priestly Prayer of the Blessing you can begin to tap into a portion of heaven coming into your life now! In the very presence of the Father you receive what the Father has! He brings with Him heaven's atmosphere. In heaven there is...

+ No limitation!

+ No sickness!

+ No oppression, depression, or emotional upheaval!

+ No warfare!

+ No lack!

+ No condemnation!

+ No murder!

+ No theft!

+ No conniving!

+ No assault and battery!

+ No injustice!

There is perfect *shalom* fulfillment, and wellness of being, prosperity, provision, love, joy, and perfection! True *shalom* is to have every part of your life brought back to completeness and to wholeness! G-D wants to restore Eden to us.

> Now may the [G-D] of hope [YHWH] fill you with all joy and peace in believing, so that you may abound in hope, through the power of the Holy Spirit [Ruach HaKodesh].
> —ROMANS 15:13

## THE SHALOM OF JERUSALEM

Pray for the peace of Jerusalem: they shall prosper that love thee.

—PSALM 122:6, KJV

To pray for Jerusalem's peace (*shalom*) is more than asking for the absence of war. It is praying that the Messiah King would return, that the holy temple will be rebuilt, the exiles will be regathered, and righteousness and holiness will prevail. It is asking that Jerusalem be restored to its original significance and importance to YHWH and His kingdom.

When a Jewish person says, "Shabbat shalom," he is saying after a long week of working and feeling drained and tired, "May the G-D of Israel restore you this Sabbath and bring about wholeness and completeness for you."

True peace (*shalom*) exists in the dwelling place of YHWH in heaven, which includes completeness and wholeness.

## BRINGING SHALOM TO EARTH

Yeshua was prophesied to be the *Sar Shalom*—in English, the Prince of Peace, which perfectly describes the ministry and personality of our Messiah.

> For unto us a child is born, unto us a son is given, and the government shall be upon his shoulder. And his name shall be called Wonderful Counselor, Mighty [G-D], Eternal Father, *Prince of Peace*.
>
> —ISAIAH 9:6

When Yeshua was born as the *Sar Shalom*—the Prince of Peace— YHWH (the heavenly Father) appeared along with the angel of the Lord in the form of the Shekinah glory!

> And in the same area [Bethlehem-Ephrata] there were shepherds living in the fields, keeping watch over their flock by night.
>
> —LUKE 2:8

Some biblical scholars today believe that these weren't average shepherds, but instead, they were Israelites who belonged to the tribe of the Levites (the priests) and were tending the sheep who were the sacrificial animals for the holy temple observances.

> And then an angel of the Lord [messenger of G-D] appeared to them, and the [Shekinah] glory of [YHWH] shone around them, and they were very afraid.
>
> —LUKE 2:9

Many theologians believe that the angel of the Lord here was part of a *theophany*—an appearance of G-D the Father Himself. The angel of the Lord was accompanied by the Shekinah glory of YHWH. In the same way that the priests were overcome and couldn't minister in the tabernacle and the holy temple when the glory came, so too the shepherds in the field were overcome by the Shekinah glory of YHWH (the heavenly Father)!

> But the angel [messenger] said to them, "Listen! Do not fear. For I bring you good news of great joy, which will be to all people."
>
> —LUKE 2:10

This was the same thing the heavenly Father said to me in my childhood dream when I beheld G-D in the form of the Shekinah glory in heaven. He said to me, "Do not be afraid, I am your friend, I will never hurt you."

> For unto you is born this day in the City of David [Bethlehem-Ephrata, which is part of greater Jerusalem] a Savior, who is Christ the Lord [Messiah Adonai].
>
> —LUKE 2:11

The heavenly Father was happy to announce the birth of His only begotten Son.

> And this will be a sign to you: You will find the Baby wrapped in strips of cloth, lying in a manger.
>
> —LUKE 2:12

A recent archaeological discovery in Bethlehem-Ephrata, which is part of greater Jerusalem, revealed a stable used by the Levitical priests to raise the sacrificial sheep and goats for the holy temple. Could it be that Yeshua (Jesus) was born in the very place where the Passover lamb and the twin male goats for the atonement offering were raised?

> Suddenly there was with the angel [messenger] a company of the heavenly host [angels] praising [YHWH] and saying, "Glory to

[YHWH] in the highest and on earth peace [shalom], and good will toward men."

—LUKE 2:13–14

The *Sar Shalom*, the promised Prince of Peace, Yeshua the Messiah was born. It will be He who, in His second coming, ushers in the "Messianic Millennial Age" when New Jerusalem descends from heaven and the glory of YHWH (our heavenly Father) fills the earth, bringing the atmosphere of heaven on the earth.

## WHEN "ULTIMATE SHALOM" INVADES EARTH

*Shalom* is an all-encompassing word for the good that comes from YHWH when He and Yeshua come to earth as New Jerusalem descends from heaven ushering in the "Messianic Age."[1]

Ultimate *shalom* will become tangible when the very atmosphere of heaven itself invades the earth. The Scriptures declare that all of creation groans for the resurrection and physical transformation of the spiritual sons and daughters of G-D.

> We know that the whole creation groans and travails in pain together until now. Not only that, but we also, who have the first fruits of the Spirit, groan within ourselves while eagerly waiting for the adoption, the redemption of our bodies.
>
> —ROMANS 8:22–23

During the Messianic Millennial Age the atmosphere on the earth and the very nature of mankind will be docile.

> Then [YHWH] will judge between many peoples and mediate for mighty nations far and wide; they will beat their swords into plowshares, and their spears into pruning hooks. Nation will not take up sword against nation, and they will no longer train for war.
>
> —MICAH 4:3

During the Messianic Millennial Age there will be such an atmosphere of *shalom* on the earth that animals that were once predators will become tame, and will no longer eat flesh, but rather, graze on the grass of the field.

The wolf also shall dwell with the lamb, and the leopard shall lie down with the young goat, and the calf and the young lion and the fatling together; and a little child shall lead them. The cow and the bear shall graze; their young ones shall lie down together; and the lion shall eat straw like the ox. The nursing child shall play by the hole of the asp, and the weaned child shall put his hand in the viper's den. They shall not hurt or destroy in all My holy mountain for the earth shall be full of the knowledge of the Lord, as the waters cover the sea. In that day there shall be a Root of Jesse [Messiah], who shall stand as a banner to the peoples. For him shall the nations seek. And his rest shall be glorious.

—Isaiah 11:6–10

In the Garden of Eden it was heaven on the earth. I believe that through G-D's divine prayer we can begin to experience a return to Eden. In the *Strong's Concordance* we see that *shalom* encompasses many different areas of our life:

*Shalom* means completeness, wholeness, health, peace, welfare, safety, soundness, tranquility, prosperity, perfectness, fullness, rest, harmony, the absence of agitation or discord. Shalom comes from the root verb *shalom* meaning to be complete, perfect and full. In modern Hebrew the obviously related word *Shelem* means "to pay for," and *Shulam* means "to be fully paid."[2]

In our English Bibles, this portion of the Priestly Prayer of the Blessing is:

…and give you *peace*.

—Numbers 6:26

The amplified Hebrew-to-English translation of this portion is:

May YHWH (YeHoVaH, YaHWeH, your heavenly Father) set in place all you need to be whole and complete so you can walk in victory, moment by moment, by the power of the Holy Spirit. May He give you supernatural health, peace, welfare, safety, soundness, tranquility, prosperity, perfection, fullness, rest, and harmony, as well as the absence of agitation and discord.

## KEYS TO THE BLESSING

When you are in the presence of YHWH (your heavenly Father) and His name (*shem*) has been placed upon you and you receive G-D's very person, His holy character, and His authority and power, you also obtain completeness and wholeness!

## STUDY QUESTIONS

In English *peace* mainly means "the absence of war," but what does the Hebrew word *shalom* mean?

_____

_____

_____

When Yeshua taught the disciples how to pray in what is referred to as the Lord's Prayer, what did He mean when He said, "Your will be done on earth, as it is in heaven?"

_____

_____

_____

What does it mean that Yeshua is referred to as the *Sar Shalom*?

_____

_____

_____

What is a theophany?

_____

_____

_____

# SECTION V:
# THE POWER OF THE PRAYER

## Chapter 19

# THE AMPLIFIED HEBREW-TO-ENGLISH TRANSLATION

GET READY TO receive the Priestly Prayer of the Blessing pronounced over you! Remember, the actual name (*shem*)—that of YHWH (your heavenly Father)—is being placed upon you through the Priestly Prayer of the Blessing. Throughout the previous section of this book I walked you through all the abstract words in the English translation of this prayer, revealing to you the deeper meaning of the original Hebrew language. Now in this chapter it is time to put it all together.

After you have proclaimed the prayer over yourself, you can also listen to the prayer being proclaimed by me in the amplified Hebrew-to-English translation and then sung over you in Hebrew by the world-renowned Messianic worship leader Paul Wilbur. Simply type this URL, www.WarrenMarcus.com/prayer, into your internet browser to access this version of the prayer being sung in either audio or video form. Both formats have been provided as a way to bless you in a powerful way.

In our English Bibles the prayer is stated in the following way:

> The LORD bless you and keep you; the LORD make His face to shine upon you, and be gracious unto you; the LORD lift His countenance upon you, and give you peace.
>
> —NUMBERS 6:24–26

Now get ready to begin receiving a supernatural impartation of the Priestly Prayer of the Blessing as you proclaim it over yourself in Hebrew in the person of, the holy character of, and the power and authority of Yeshua, the Jewish High Priest in heaven! After you pronounce the amplified Hebrew-to-English translation over yourself, pray the following prayer and continue reading this chapter.

*YHWH (Father G-D), I thank You that I can walk in Your shalom. You are the One who created the heavens and the earth. Every knee shall bow and every tongue shall confess Your name and the name of Your Son. Father, I thank You. I receive now Your name placed upon me, meaning Your person, Your character, Your authority, and Your supernatural power. Help me, YHWH, to demonstrate to others who You are so they too can experience Your reality. Amen.*

---

יְבָרֶכְךָ יְהֹוָה וְיִשְׁמְרֶךָ׃

**The LORD bless you, and keep you;**

יָאֵר יְהֹוָה פָּנָיו אֵלֶיךָ וִיחֻנֶּךָּ׃

**The LORD make His face shine on you, And be gracious to you;**

יִשָּׂא יְהֹוָה פָּנָיו אֵלֶיךָ וְיָשֵׂם לְךָ שָׁלוֹם׃

**The LORD lift up His countenance on you, And give you peace.**

---

In our English Bibles it reads:

The LORD *bless* you...

But in my amplified Hebrew-to-English translation of the prayer it is:

May YHWH (YeHoVaH, YaHWeH) kneel before you (making Himself available to you as your heavenly Father) so He can grant or bestow upon you His promises and gifts.

In the first portion of the Priestly Prayer of the Blessing YHWH kneels in front of you, His spiritual son or daughter, as a good parent desiring to make Himself available and minister to you. This requires a response. Do you keep standing, or do you humble yourself and kneel in front of Him?

In our English Bibles it reads:

The LORD bless you and *keep* you...

But in my amplified translation of the prayer it is:

May YHWH (YeHoVaH, YaHWeH, your heavenly Father) guard you with a hedge of thorny protection that will prevent Satan and all your enemies from harming your body, soul, mind, and spirit, your loved ones, and all your possessions.

In this second portion your heavenly Father places His arms around you with a divine embrace, holding you in His strong arms of protection and security.

In our English Bibles it reads:

The LORD make His *face* to shine upon you...

But in my amplified Hebrew-to-English translation of the prayer it is:

May YHWH (YeHoVaH, YaHWeH, your heavenly Father) illuminate the wholeness of His being toward you, continually bringing to you order, so that you will fulfill your G-D-given destiny and purpose.

In this portion of the Priestly Prayer of the Blessing it's as if He loosens His divine embrace and while still keeping His holy hands upon your shoulders, He pulls away enough for you to see Him face-to-face so you can begin to experience His reality and person.

In our English Bibles it reads:

And be *gracious* unto you...

But in my amplified translation it is:

May YHWH (YeHoVaH, YaHWeH, your heavenly Father) provide you with perfect love and fellowship, never leaving you, and give you sustenance, provision, and friendship.

Your heavenly Father reveals His perfect love to you as your perfect Daddy with loving eyes and a beatific smile. He looks past your weaknesses and your frailties, pledging that He will never leave you and that He will provide you with His love, fellowship, and friendship. It is your heavenly Father saying to you, "You are my beloved son or daughter, in whom I am well pleased."

In our English Bibles it reads:

The Lord *lift* His countenance upon you…

But in my amplified Hebrew-to-English translation of the prayer it is:

May YHWH (YeHoVaH, YaHWeH, your heavenly Father) lift up and carry His fullness of being toward you (bringing everything that He has to your aid), supporting you with His divine embrace and His entire being.

This is your heavenly Father lifting you up with His divine strong arms and carrying you, continually looking down at you as He walks. He is your loving heavenly Father.

He is also lifting up *all of who He is* toward you. He is putting all of Himself at your disposal. He is bringing everything that He is to your aid. He is supporting you with *His entire being*. Nothing is being withheld. You have the one true G-D of the universe on your side!

In our English Bibles it reads:

And give you *peace*…

But in my amplified Hebrew-to-English translation it is:

May YHWH (YeHoVaH, YaHWeH, your heavenly Father) set in place all you need to be whole and complete so you can walk in victory, moment by moment, by the power of the Holy Spirit. May He give you supernatural health, peace, welfare, safety, soundness, tranquility, prosperity, perfection, fullness, rest, and harmony, as well as the absence of agitation and discord.

## HOW TO PRONOUNCE THE DIVINE PRAYER OVER YOURSELF AND OTHERS

Now that you have pronounced the Priestly Prayer of the Blessing over yourself and then had it sung over you in Hebrew by listening to the audio or video recording on my website, you also can pronounce this over yourself and others every day!

In order for you to administer this divine prayer over others in the manner prescribed by YHWH, you must be sure that you are born again. If you are not sure that you have been born again, you can say the prayers in chapter 5 as an example, or simply pray (talk to G-D) in your own words that express what you feel in your heart.

Now that you are truly born again, and you have been made an adopted son or daughter of the one true G-D of Israel, you can effectively pronounce this prayer over yourself and others every day. Yeshua is your High Priest, and He wants to say the Priestly Prayer of the Blessing over you every day!

## WHAT YOU ARE ABOUT TO DO IS SUPERNATURAL!

As you speak out loud over yourself this amplified Hebrew-to-English translation of the Priestly Prayer of the Blessing, it will be your voice speaking, but by proxy it will be Yeshua Himself in heaven speaking it through your mouth.

Your ears will hear the prayer of blessing. Your mind will be washed and regenerated through this prayer. Supernaturally the name of the one true G-D of Israel, YHWH (YeHoVaH, YaHWeH, your heavenly Father) will be supernaturally placed upon you. To have His name (*shem*) supernaturally placed upon you means the one true G-D of Israel's very breath, the essence of who the bearer of the name truly is, His very person, His holy character, and His power and authority will be supernaturally imparted to you.

Now continue to pray this amplified Hebrew-to-English translation of the prayer out loud every day.

# CONCLUSION

THROUGHOUT MY JOURNEY and discovery concerning the Priestly Prayer of the Blessing I would update my friend Rick Amato about my findings. It was because of him that I began my quest to understand the truth about G-D's divine prayer of the blessing.

When I finally sent Rick the amplified Hebrew-to-English translation of the prayer and the audio recording of it being sung in Hebrew, he was overwhelmed. He shared with me that now he too has experienced the name of the one true G-D of Israel upon him. Though he had been withdrawn from ministry for several years, he now has received a yearning and passion to preach again and make the name of G-D known to the nations!

Rick wrote me:

Dear Warren,

All my adult life I have told you amazing stories from across the globe about my life that, if they hadn't happened to you and I together, I'm not sure, either of us would ever believe any of them. We've come to know these God-sent miracles with the word Albert Einstein used—*synchronicity*. Well, here is one more. This one may be the most amazing and life changing yet. And it is a direct result of your faithfulness and holy devotion to the one true [G-D] of your fathers (you are my favorite rabbi) in deciphering that pendant the Israelis gave me.

Not that long ago, I was simply listening to the audio CD of the Priestly Prayer of the Blessing you spoke over me, and the amazingly beautiful way it was sung in the Hebrew. It occurred to me how much I have not only survived against all odds, but found enormous prosperity and above all a heart full of perfect peace! A warm feeling of serenity, peace, and inner prosperity washed over me again and again. Never have I experienced anything like it. I thought, "So this is the [G-D] of Abraham, Isaac, and Jacob, the [G-D] my earthly daddy Emanueli called, the 'Great I AM'?"

My next thought was "I've led over a million people in forty-nine countries to have faith in the [G-D] of Israel through Jesus Christ. I've memorized the entire New Testament and large portions of the Old—and I missed this?" Then it dawned on me that none of it was ever about me or my name anyway. It was about hallowing [G-D] the Father's name because that's where His character and person is. It's about the Father heart of [G-D]. Then I thought of my precious daughter, Beth Anne.

You know Beth Anne loved and believed in you, Warren. After that first dinner with you she said "Daddy, I've been all over the world with you and met every kind of person but that man is the real deal with [G-D]." She was just an eighteen-year-old kid then. You can kid a fool, but you can't fool a kid.

No words will ever be able to describe the purity and honest compassion of her heart and life. Only a little over two and a half years since her death now, her devotion to her three sons and the elementary school children she taught and freely served is the stuff of legend at the school. To be her father was to have my name honored and loved. She always sought to live up to her last name no matter what. She literally was only disciplined once in her entire life and was the one kid that lived all that I nurtured her and trained her to be. The hospital tragedy that claimed her life left me despairing to see another day on earth and having to force myself to breathe. She was my firstborn, my baby. To lose any child is the greatest sorrow a human can know in this life. To lose this kind of child is an unspeakable tragedy.

Now, Warren, you know I see myself as a man of science and not easily given over to religious experiences. Not that long ago, however, I had one that was not from this world. All I can say is that after the worst trouble a human can endure on earth, now, instead of dying with my precious baby Bethie, *I want to live for her*. More than that, I want to live purely for the Father who is represented in the blessing spoken over me. I want to honor my heavenly Father's name whose breath has touched my spirit and made me new again. I want to show the world what you've been trying to tell me about the Fatherhood of the Almighty for all of humankind.

I've made a new choice to live simply to honor the blessed name of the one true [G-D] (YHWH) by being the person and character of authenticity He deserves. I want to honor His name instead of my own name. Ever since I began listening to and trying to follow the teachings you are disseminating about the sacred Hebrew name nothing remains unblessed in my life. The audio CD with the Hebrew chanting of this divine prayer and the pronouncement of the Priestly Prayer of the Blessing took me into an entirely new unfathomable level of intimacy and personal authenticity with my heavenly Father. Thank you with all my heart, Warren.

The presence and power of Providence in my life through this spiritual experience made me think of something else: *Could it be a divine synchronicity that while the Israeli people gave me that pendant, the first replica, as a token of gratitude for helping tens of thousands of Jewish people leave the former Soviet Union and immigrate to Israel when the USSR fell—could it be that it was because [G-D] knew you, Warren, would decipher its secret code, which in turn would revolutionize my life as a grieving father when no one else could help me?*

Over time we will see, and over time the truth always comes out. What I did not know and what has transformed my life and set me back on the path of an inner healing and delight of life, is what I'm learning now about the power to be 100 percent authentic that studying the character and person of the sacred name can give a human being. I've experienced its outer power for a lifetime with [G-D's] Spirit *upon* me. Today, I feel rocketed into another dimension as I am learning through His name the power He placed within me!

This, I think, is going to be the key to all future understanding of the significance of the Bible. It is also validation of what I've said for so long now, that it is impossible to understand Jesus the Messiah outside of the Jewish context.

Warren, after five "study trips" to Israel and forty years of seeking to understand the one true [G-D], because of the teachings I have received from you about the character and person of the name, I might finally be beginning to be onto something completely real here. Perhaps that is why the incredibly astronomical odds against me ever getting that thirty-nine-year-old file, which was returned to me all the way from the Far East, proves that divine providence has a way of accomplishing certain objectives among humans.

Providence no doubt gave me you as a friend. I'm more thankful that since Beth's death, the blessing of knowing you as a teacher and preacher has helped me to recover my authentic sense of self as a child of the Most High [G-D]. If it can happen for me, it can happen for anyone—no matter who they are or what they've done. My life will never be the same. Blessed be the Name.

Your Fellow Servant,

Rick Amato

# PHOTO SECTION

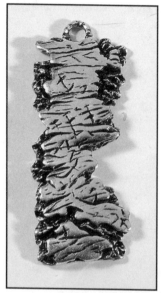

Authorized replica of the ancient pendant inscribed with the Priestly Prayer of the Blessing found in 1979.

Archaeology site opposite the Temple Mount in Jerusalem where the amulet (pendant) was found in 1979 by archaeologist Gabriel Barkay. Photo by Shmuel Browns.

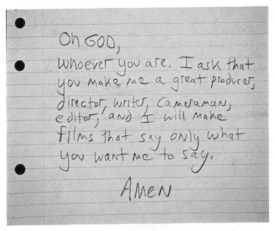

Prayer Warren wrote and prayed to G-D after
seeing *The Ten Commandments* movie.

Warren on the movie set producing the highest-rated religious
prime-time TV special for CBN, *Don't Ask Me, Ask God.*

Poster of the animated series *SuperBook*, which Warren produced for CBN.

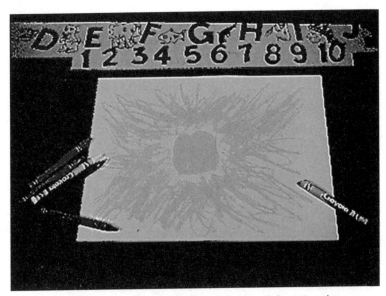

The picture that five-year-old Warren colored depicting the
dream he had when he saw the Shekinah glory of G-D.

Warren filming the authorized documentary of the
Brownsville Revival in Pensacola, Florida.

Warren has received more than thirty-five awards for the various religious programs and films he has produced, including Clio, Telly, Religion in Media, and New York Film Festival.

Authorized replica of the amulet or pendant with the Priestly Prayer of the Blessing etched in Paleo-Hebrew on the front and English on the back.

The divine prayer on the silver amulet (or pendant) discovered
in 1979 by Gabriel Barkay. It is the oldest evidence of Holy
Scripture etched into silver in Paleo-Hebrew.
Photo © The Israel Museum, Jerusalem, by Nahum Slapak

Evangelist Rick Amato called Warren after the Priestly Prayer
of the Blessing was prayed over him in Jerusalem.

Warren on the archaeologist site of the synagogue in
Capernaum, Israel, where Yeshua (Jesus) preached).

Warren at three months old with his sister, Fran, who first told him about the existence of G-D and heaven.

Warren at three years old being held by his teenage sister, Fran, who became a believer in Yeshua as her Messiah through Warren's witness to her.

Rick Amato with his daughter Beth Anne Amato, who will
always be remembered for her caring Christian heart.

# NOTES

## CHAPTER 1
### AN AMAZING DISCOVERY

1. "About Dr. Gabriel Barkay," Gabriel Barkay.com, accessed September 1, 2017, http://www.gabrielbarkay.com/about-dr-barkay.html.
2. "About Dr. Gabriel Barkay."

## CHAPTER 3
### HOW TO ACCESS THE FULL IMPARTATION

1. "The Culture of the Bible: Understanding the Bible Through Hebrew Culture," December 5, 2012, https://biblicalculture.wordpress.com/2012/12/05/the-four-levels-of-interpretation/.

## CHAPTER 4
### WHAT IS THE SHEKINAH GLORY?

1. Yiddish Book Center, "Live Long and Prosper: The Jewish Story Behind Spock, Leonard Nimoy's Star Trek Character," YouTube video, posted February 4, 2014, https://youtu.be/DyiWkWcR86I; https://www.youtube.com/watch?v=UdYbpMkH_XQ&feature=youtu.be; Uncle Spellbinder, "The Birth of "Live Long and Prosper," YouTube video, posted December 15, 2016, https://www.youtube.com/watch?v=UdYbpMkH_XQ&feature=youtu.be.
2. Yiddish Book Center, "Live Long and Prosper"; Uncle Spellbinder, "The Birth of "Live Long and Prosper."

## CHAPTER 6
### THE POWER OF THE HEBREW LANGUAGE

1. Cyndi Dale, The Subtle Body: An Encyclopedia of Your Energetic Anatomy (Boulder, CO: Sounds True, 2009).

## CHAPTER 8
### THE SACRED NAME

1. M. J. Afshari, "Is Allah the Same God as the God of the Bible?," The Interactive Bible, accessed November 22, 2017, http://www.bible.ca/islam/library/islam-quotes-afshari.htm.

2. Andrew Jukes, *The Names of God in Holy Scripture* (Whitefish, MT: Kessinger Publishing, 1889); "I AM who AM," Catholic Answers Forums, accessed December 22, 2017, https://forums.catholic.com/t/i -am-who-am/43150; Ken Burns, "The Proper Name of the Creator," Bible researcher, accessed December 22, 2017, http://bibleresearcher .com/fellowship-with-god-01.html; "Exodus 3:14 God's Name I AM— Septuagint ego eimi—in Different Languages," Bjorkbloggen, posted March 8, 2014, https://bjorkbloggen.com/2014/03/08/exodus -314-gods-name-i-am-septuagint-ego-eimi-in-different-languages/.
3. Nate Sullivan, "Omnipotent, Omniscient and Omnipresent God: Definition & Overview," Study.com, accessed November 24, 2017, http:// study.com/academy/lesson/omnipotent-omniscient-and-omnipresent -god-definition-lesson-quiz.html.
4. Sullivan, "Omnipotent, Omniscient and Omnipresent God."

## CHAPTER 10
## THE HEBREW WORD FOR BLESS

1. Howard Schwartz, *Tree of Souls: The Mythology of Judaism* (Oxford: Oxford University Press, 2006).

## CHAPTER 11
## THE HEBREW WORD FOR KEEP

1. Peggy Joyce Ruth and Angela Ruth Schum, *Psalm 91* (Lake Mary, FL: Charisma House, 2010).

## CHAPTER 12
## THE HEBREW WORD FOR FACE

1. *Funk and Wagnall's Standard Desk Dictionary* (New York: Funk and Wagnall Inc., 1976), s.v. "compassion."
2. "Show Me Your Face" by Don Potter © 1996 Sheep In Tow Music, used with permission. To purchase this song or access other music by Don Potter, go to www.potterhausmusic.net.

## CHAPTER 13
## THE HEBREW WORD FOR SHINE

1. Reference.com, "What Is the Biblical Meaning of the Word 'Restoration?,'" IAC Publishing, LLC, accessed December 18, 2017, https:// www.reference.com/world-view/biblical-meaning-word-restoration -436ed0eb2e3b3d0c#.

## CHAPTER 16
## THE HEBREW WORD FOR COUNTENANCE

1. Rhiannon Lloyd and Joseph Nyamutera, *Healing the Wounds of Ethnic Conflict* (Geneva, Switzerland: Mercy Ministries International, 2010), accessed November 26, 2017, www.lerucher.org/Content/pdf /Knowing%20G-D%20as%20Loving%20Father.pdf.

## CHAPTER 17
## THE HEBREW WORD FOR GIVE

1. StudyLight.org, s.v. "*siym*," accessed November 26, 2017, https://www .studylight.org/lexicons/hebrew/7760.html.
2. Claire Bates, "Scientists Find Couples' Vital Signs Mimic Each Other," *Daily Mail*, February 12, 2013, http://www.dailymail.co.uk/health /article-2277586/Two-hearts-really-DO-beat-youre-love-Scientists -couples-vital-signs-mimic-other.html.

## CHAPTER 18
## THE HEBREW WORD FOR PEACE

1. "Peace-Shalom (Hebrew Word Study)," Precept Austin, August 20, 2016, http://www.preceptaustin.org/shalom_-_definition.
2. Strong's Concordance, s.v. "shalom,"

# WARREN M. MARCUS

WARREN HAS BEEN a Messianic Jewish believer since October 1974. He is ordained as a Spirit-filled evangelist in the Southern Baptist denomination. Today he serves as vice president of Sid Roth's Messianic Vision Inc., where he oversees the radio and television productions, including the weekly *It's Supernatural!* television show.

Warren pastors a weekly One New Man (Creation) Meeting every Saturday at 6:00 p.m. at Steele Creek Church of Charlotte in North Carolina. His teaching of the Hebrew roots has helped many in the church today enter into a deeper relationship with the G-D of Israel and Jesus the Messiah.

Warren has produced the Great North American Revival DVD series, which features his award-winning documentaries on the Toronto Blessing, the Smithton Outpouring, and the Brownsville Revival. While filming these documentaries, he was profoundly impacted, and he shares what he learned about these great moves of G-D. The series includes rare anointed footage from these great revivals. People who have watched these videos have reported the glory of G-D invading their homes!

Warren is known for his award-winning productions, including the Christian Broadcasting Network's animated Bible stories for children *SuperBook* and *Flying House*. He also produced the highest-rated religious TV special of all time, *Don't Ask Me, Ask God*. It featured Hollywood stars such as Michael J. Fox, Ned Beatty, and others. This prime-time TV special garnered a 10.5 Nielsen TV rating with an audience of over sixteen million people.

# GET THE ENTIRE COURSE!

**Includes:**

- **2-PART AUDIO CD TEACHING** (over 2 hours of anointed teaching)

- **WORK BOOK** (which helps guide you through the teaching)

- **FRAMABLE PRINT** of the AMPLIFIED Hebrew-to-English "Ancient Priestly Prayer

  of the Blessing"

- **The BLESSING PENDANT with NECKLACE** (a Replica of the Pendant which includes the

  PRAYER in the Ancient Paleo-Hebrew as it was discovered on the original and the English

  Translation of the prayer on the back of the Pendant.

- **PAMPHLET** with teaching about the Blessing Pendant

**To order go to:**

www.warrenmarcus.com

# Priestly Prayer of the Blessing
### (Numbers 6:24-26)

יְבָרֶכְךָ יְהוָה וְיִשְׁמְרֶךָ:

**The LORD bless you, and keep you;**

יָאֵר יְהוָה פָּנָיו אֵלֶיךָ וִיחֻנֶּךָ:

**The LORD make His face shine on you, And be gracious to you;**

יִשָּׂא יְהוָה פָּנָיו אֵלֶיךָ וְיָשֵׂם לְךָ שָׁלוֹם:

**The LORD lift up His countenance on you, And give you peace.**

## Amplified Hebrew to English Interpretation

**THE LORD BLESS YOU...**
May YHWH (HE who exists) KNEEL BEFORE YOU presenting GIFTS.

**AND KEEP YOU...**
GUARD YOU with a HEDGE of THORNY protection that will prevent Satan and all your enemies from harming you. May HE protect your body, soul, mind, spirit, your loved ones and all your possessions!

**THE LORD MAKE HIS FACE SHINE UPON YOU...**
May YHWH (HE who exists) illuminate the WHOLENESS of HIS BEING toward you continually bringing ORDER, so that you will fulfill your God-given destiny and purpose.

**AND BE GRACIOUS TO YOU...**
May YHWH (HE who exists) provide you with PERFECT LOVE and FELLOWSHIP (never leaving you) and give you SUSTENANCE (provision) and FRIENDSHIP.

**THE LORD LIFT HIS COUNTENANCE ON YOU...**
May YHWH (HE who exists) LIFT UP and CARRY His WHOLENESS of being toward you (bringing everything that He is to YOUR aid – supporting YOU with His ENTIRE BEING).

**AND GIVE YOU PEACE...**
And may YHWH (HE who exists) set in place all you need to be WHOLE and COMPLETE so you can walk in victory, moment by moment, by the power of the Holy Spirit. May HE give you supernatural health, peace, welfare, safety, soundness, tranquility, prosperity, perfection, fullness, rest, harmony, as well as, the absence of agitation and discord.

# DISPLAY IT

**Includes: A FRAMABLE PRINT** of the AMPLIFIED Hebrew-to-English "Ancient Priestly Prayer of the Blessing".

**To order go to:**

www.warrenmarcus.com

# WEAR IT